PROGRESSIVE

Guitar

FOR BEGINNERS

By Gary Turner &
Peter Gelling

PROGRESSIVE GUITAR
I.S.B.N. 978-982-9118-18-9
Order Code: 11818

For more information on
this series contact:
L.T.P. Publishing Pty Ltd
email: info@learntoplaymusic.com
or visit our website:
www.learntoplaymusic.com

Published by
KOALA MUSIC PUBLICATIONS ™

Contents

Contents Continued

Contents Continued

Other Titles by Koala Music Publications

Koala Music Publications has a large variety of music instruction books including a whole series of Guitar Methods and comprehensive Guitar Manuals. While you are studying this book, you will find *Progressive Guitar Method: Theory* particularly useful. On completion of this book, you will be ready to study specific types of guitar playing such as Rhythm, Lead, and Fingerpicking.

Shown below are some of the other titles published by Koala Music Publications.

Beginner Basics Guitar Bible

An indispensable self-teaching, learning and reference manual for the beginning Guitarist. Hardcover, Glossy Full Colour, 332-page manual with 90 lessons covering Lead, Rhythm and Fingerpicking styles. Contains 5DVDs, and DVD-rom with over 570 audio and 350 video files to download to PC, Mac, iPod or MP3 player.

Progressive Guitar for Adults

52 Full colour, step-by-step lessons to learn to play any style of guitar. Covers both melody and chord playing including both open position and moveable shapes along with all the essential techniques for both rhythm and lead guitar playing. Also covers understanding rhythms, scales and keys and how to write your own music. All examples sound great and are fun to play.

Progressive Guitar Method: Lead

Covers scales and patterns over the entire fretboard so that you can improvise against major, minor, and Blues progressions in any key. Learn the licks and techniques used by all lead guitarists such as hammer-ons, slides, bending, vibrato, and more.

Progressive Guitar Method: Fingerpicking

Introduces right hand fingerpicking patterns that can be used as an accompaniment to any chord, chord progression or song. Covers alternate thumb, arpeggio and constant bass styles as used in Rock, Pop, Folk, Country, Blues Ragtime and Classical music.

Progressive Guitar Method: Chords

Contains the most useful open, Bar and Jazz chord shapes of the most used chord types with chord progressions to practice and play along with. Includes sections on tuning, how to read sheet music, transposing, as well as an easy chord table, formula and symbol chart.

Progressive Guitar Method: Bar Chords

Introduces the most useful Bar, Rock and Jazz chord shapes used by all Rock/Pop/ Country and Blues guitarists. Includes major, minor, seventh, sixth, major seventh, etc. Suggested rhythm patterns including percussive strums, dampening and others are also covered.

Progressive Guitar Method: Book 2

A comprehensive, lesson by lesson method covering the most important keys and scales for guitar, with special emphasis on bass note picking, bass note runs, hammer-ons etc. Featuring chordal arrangements of well known Rock, Blues, Folk and Traditional songs.

Progressive Guitar Method: Theory

A comprehensive introduction to music theory as it applies to the guitar. Covers reading traditional music, rhythm notation and tablature, along with learning the notes on the fretboard, how to construct chords and scales, transposition, musical terms and playing in all keys.

Introduction

Progressive GUITAR assumes you have no prior knowledge of music or playing the GUITAR.
Starting from the types of guitar available and the different styles of playing you are introduced to :

1.   Important basic chord shapes and chord progressions.
2.   Learn to read and play guitar music using standard music notation, EASY READ TAB and EASY READ strumming patterns and chord diagrams.
3.   Learn to play the notes on all six strings.
4.   Learn the melodies and chords of many well known songs along with great sounding original melodies and chord progressions in a variety of contemporary styles including Rock, Blues, Funk, Country and World Music.
5.   Learn basic music theory including time signatures, sharps and flats, major scales etc.
6.   Learn the most common open chord shapes in the keys of C major, G major and A minor.

The book also has special sections on tuning, how to play in a band, how to read sheet music of your favourite groups, and a chord chart.

After completing this book you will have a solid understanding of the guitar and will be ready for further study on specific styles of guitar playing.

All guitarists should know all of the information contained in this book.
The best and fastest way to learn is to use this book in conjunction with:
1.   Buying sheet music and song books of your favourite recording artists and learning to play their songs.
2.   Practicing and playing with other musicians. You will be surprised how good a basic drums/bass/ guitar combination can sound even when playing easy music.
3.   Learning by listening to your favourite CDs.

Also in the early stages it is helpful to have the guidance of an experienced teacher. This will also help you keep to a schedule and obtain weekly goals.

Approach to Practice

It is important to have a correct approach to practice. You will benefit more from several short practices (e.g. 15-30 minutes per day) than one or two long sessions per week. This is especially so in the early stages, because of the basic nature of the material being studied. In a practice session you should divide your time evenly between the study of new material and the revision of past work. It is a common mistake for semi-advanced students to practice only the pieces they can already play well. Although this is more enjoyable, it is not a very satisfactory method of practice. You should also try to correct mistakes and experiment with new ideas. It is the authors' belief that an experienced teacher will be an invaluable aid to your progress.

Using the Accompanying DVDs, DVD-ROM and CD

The accompanying discs contain video and audio recordings of the examples in this book. An exercise number and a play icon on a colored strip indicates a recorded example:

 57 ← **CD TRACK / DVD MENU NUMBER**

The book shows you where to put your fingers and what techniques to use, and the recordings let you hear and see how each example should sound and look when performed correctly.

DVD Angle Option 1

Practice the examples slowly at first on your own. Then try playing to a metronome set to a slow tempo, such that you can play the example evenly and without stopping. Gradually increase the tempo as you become more confident and then you can try playing along with the recording.

You will hear a drum beat at the beginning of each example, to lead you into the example and to help you keep time.

Your guitar must be in tune with the recordings to play along (see the "Tuning Your Guitar" section at the end of the book).

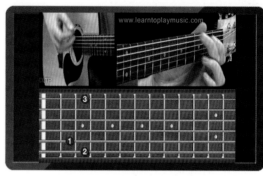
DVD Angle Option 2

Included with this book:

* **2 DVDs**, which can be played in any DVD player and contain all the exercises in this book with multiple camera angles, fretboard animations and full scrolling scores (displayed above). These are accessed from your DVD player remote using the video angle button available on most DVD players. Also, you can choose between several audio options including 'main part with backing track' (so you can hear how the guitar should sound with a band), 'solo main part' (so you can hear the guitar by itself) or 'backing track only' (so you can play along). These audio angles (or language tracks) are also accessed from the DVD remote.

* **1 DVD-ROM**, which can be used in any computer and most gaming consoles and portable media players (e.g. iPod, Xbox, Playstation etc) and contains all the audio and video for all exercises in this book. Both discs contain identical content but one is for use with Microsoft Windows Media Player (included free with all Windows PCs) and the other for Apple iTunes and Quicktime Media Player (included free with all Apple Mac computers and available for Windows PCs via free download at www.apple.com). On both discs you will find two folders, one containing the video examples and the other containing the audio examples. Follow the instructions for your media player to import these files to your hard drive and transfer to your portable media player if required.

* **1 CD**, which can be played in any CD player. Due to the limitations of the CD format not all examples are present on the CD.

Tips

* Most CD, DVD and portable media players have the ability to repeat tracks. You can make good use of this feature to practice the examples a number of times without stopping.

* The latest versions of both Windows Media Player and Quicktime Player (available with iTunes) have the ability to slow down the speed of the recorded exercises while still maintaining the correct pitch. This is very handy for practicing the more complex pieces.

Electronic Tuner

The easiest and most accurate way to tune your guitar is by using an **electronic tuner**. An electronic tuner allows you to tune each string individually to the tuner, by indicating whether the notes are sharp (too high) or flat (too low). If you have an electric guitar you can plug it directly into the tuner. If you have an acoustic guitar the tuner will have an inbuilt microphone. There

Electronic Tuner

are several types of electronic guitar tuners but most are relatively inexpensive and simple to operate. Tuning using other methods is difficult for beginning guitarists and it takes many months to master, so we recommend you purchase an electronic tuner, particularly if you do not have a guitar teacher or a friend who can tune it for you. Also if your guitar is way out of tune you can always take it to your local music store so they can tune it for you. Once a guitar has been tuned correctly it should only need minor adjustments before each practice session. To learn to tune the guitar using other methods see page 164.

Tuning Your Guitar to the Recording

Before you commence each lesson or practice session you will need to tune your guitar. If your guitar is out of tune everything you play will sound incorrect even though you are holding the correct notes. On the accompanying CD, the first track has a recording of each of the six strings of the guitar. These are also on the DVD and the DVD-ROM. For a complete description of how to tune your guitar, see page 164.

 1.0 **6th String**
E Note (Thickest string)

 1.1 **5th String**
A Note

 1.2 **4th String**
D Note

 1.3 **3rd String**
G Note

 1.4 **2nd String**
B Note

 1.5 **1st String**
E Note (Thinnest string)

Acoustic Guitars

Classical Guitar
(Nylon Strings)

Steel String Acoustic

The **classical guitar** has nylon strings and a wider neck than other types of guitar. It is most commonly used for playing Classical, Flamenco and Fingerstyles. Generally it is much cheaper than other types of guitar and is recommended for beginning guitarists.

The **steel string acoustic** has steel strings and is most commonly played by strumming or fingerpicking groups of notes called chords. This is the type of acoustic guitar you will hear in most modern styles of music e.g. Acoustic Rock, Pop, Folk, Country, Blues and World music.

Electric Guitars

Electric guitars have **pick-ups** (a type of inbuilt microphone) and need to be played into an **amplifier** (amp) to be heard.

The **solid body electric** is commonly used in Metal, Rock, Blues and Pop. Famous solid body guitars are the **Gibson Les Paul** and the **Fender Stratocaster**.

The **hollow body electric** (semi acoustic) is most commonly used in Jazz and Blues.

Acoustic guitars can be amplified by placing a microphone near the sound hole or by placing a portable pick-up on the body of the guitar. This is common for performances at large venues where the acoustic guitar needs amplification to be heard.

Electric Guitars *(PLAYED THROUGH AN AMPLIFIER)*

Solid Body Electric
Hollow Body Electric
(semi acoustic)

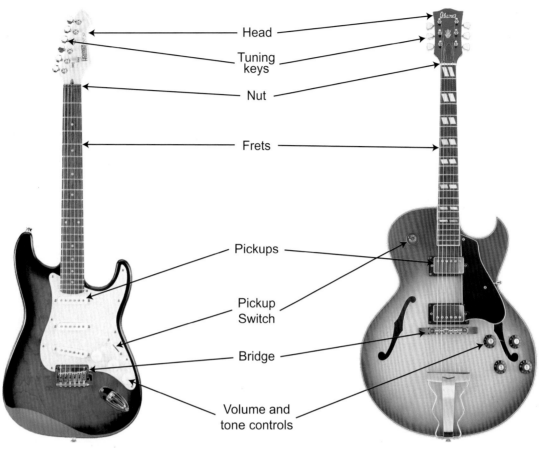

Head

Tuning keys

Nut

Frets

Pickups

Pickup Switch

Bridge

Volume and tone controls

Amplifiers

Combo
(combined amp and speaker)

Stack
(separate amp head and speaker)

Strings

It is important to have the correct set of strings fitted to your guitar, especially if you are a beginner. Until you build enough strength in your hands to fret the chords cleanly, light gauge or low tension strings are recommended. A reputable music store which sells guitar strings should be able to assist with this. Do not put steel strings on a classical guitar as they will damage the neck of the guitar. It is important to change your strings regularly, as old strings go out of tune easily and are more difficult to keep in tune.

Seating

Before you commence playing, a comfortable seating position is required. Most modern guitarists prefer to sit with their right leg raised, (as shown in the photo) or by placing their right foot on a footstool. The guitar should be close to the body, and in a vertical position. The main aim is for comfort and easy access to the guitar. A music stand will also be helpful.

Standing

1   Use a wide guitar strap and adjust it to a comfortable length. Let the strap take the weight of the guitar. This will keep your hands free to play rather than having to support the instrument.
2   Make sure your weight is balanced evenly between both feet.
3   The guitar should sit comfortably against your body in an upright position, with the neck pointing slightly upwards.

The standing position is particularly good for playing electric guitar and is essential if you plan to play in a band. Once you are comfortable with this position, try moving in time with the music as you play.

Right Hand and Arm

Using the Pick

The right hand is used to play the strings by plucking them with a pick.
A pick is a piece of plastic shaped like a triangle.

Hold the pick lightly between your thumb and first finger, as shown in the following photo.

Use the tip of the pick to play the string.

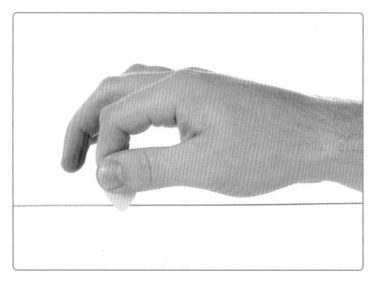

Right Arm Position

The correct position for the right arm is illustrated in **Photo A** below. Notice that the fore-arm rests on the upper edge of the guitar, just below the elbow. Be careful not to have the elbow hanging over the face of the guitar or your hand too far along the fretboard (**Photo B**).

Photo A: CORRECT

Photo B: INCORRECT

The Left Hand

The left hand fingers are numbered as such:

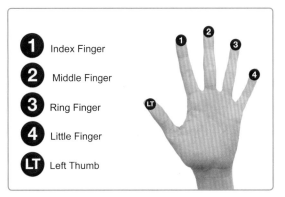

1 Index Finger
2 Middle Finger
3 Ring Finger
4 Little Finger
LT Left Thumb

Left Hand Placement

Your fingers should be **on their tips** and placed just **left** of the frets (not on top of them).

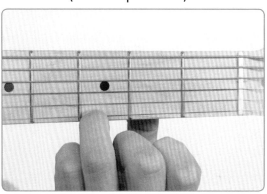

Be careful not to allow the thumb to hang too far over the top of the neck (**Photo C**), or to let it run parallel along the back of the neck (**Photo D**).

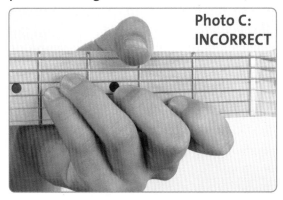

Photo C: INCORRECT

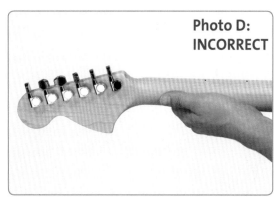

Photo D: INCORRECT

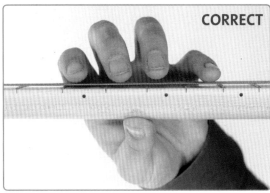

CORRECT

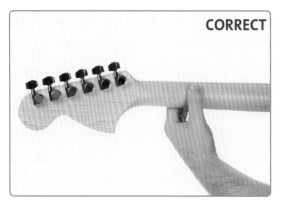

CORRECT

How to Read Music

There are two methods used to write guitar music: **traditional music notation** method (using music notes, ♩) and **tablature.** Both are used in this book but you need only use one of these methods. Most guitarists find Tablature easier to read, but it is important to learn to read traditional music notation as well. Nearly all sheet music you buy in a store is written in traditional notation.

Tablature

Tablature is a method of indicating the position of notes on the fretboard. There are six "tab" lines each representing one of the six strings of the guitar. Study the following diagram.

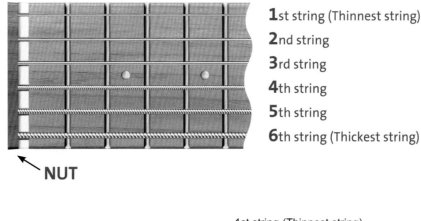

A number placed on one of the lines indicates the fret location of a note.

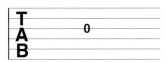   This indicates the open 3rd string (a G note).

   This indicates the 3rd fret of the 5th string (a C note).

   This indicates the 1st fret of the 1st string (an F note).

The Rudiments of Music

The musical alphabet consists of 7 letters:

A B C D E F G

Music is written on a **staff**, which consists of 5 parallel lines between which there are 4 spaces.

Music Staff

The treble or 'G' clef is placed at the beginning of each staff line. This clef indicates the position of the note G. (It is an old fashioned method of writing the letter G, with the centre of the clef being written on the second staff line.)

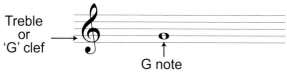

The other lines and spaces on the staff are named as such:

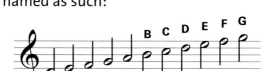

Extra notes can be added by the use of short lines, called **leger lines**.

When a note is placed on the staff its head indicates its position, e.g.:

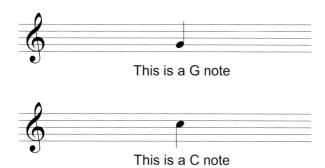

This is a G note

This is a C note

When the note head is below the middle staff line the stem points upward and when the head is above the middle line the stem points downward. A note placed on the middle line (**B**) can have its stem pointing either up or down.

Bar lines are drawn across the staff, which divides the music into sections called **bars** or **measures**. A **double bar line** signifies either the end of the music, or the end of an important section of it.

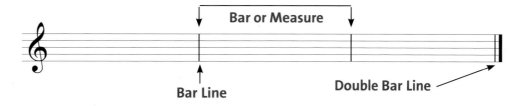

Bar or Measure

Bar Line

Double Bar Line

Note Values

The following table sets out the most common notes used in music and their respective time values (i.e. length of time held). For each note value there is an equivalent rest, which indicates a period of silence.

Whole Note and Rest (Semibreve)	Half Note and Rest (Minim)	Quarter Note and Rest (Crotchet)	Eighth Note and Rest (Quaver)	Sixteenth Note and Rest (Semiquaver)

4	2	1	1/2	1/4

If a **DOT** is placed after a note it increases the value of that note by half, e.g.

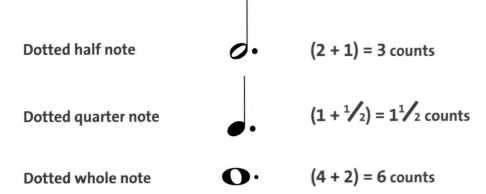

Dotted half note		(2 + 1) = 3 counts
Dotted quarter note		$(1 + \frac{1}{2}) = 1\frac{1}{2}$ counts
Dotted whole note		(4 + 2) = 6 counts

A **tie** is a curved line joining two or more notes of the same pitch, where the second note(s) **is note played** but its time value is added to that of the first note. Here are two examples:

In both of these examples only the first note is played.

Time Signatures

At the beginning of each piece of music, after the treble clef, is the **time signature**.

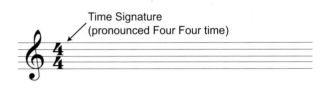

Time Signature
(pronounced Four Four time)

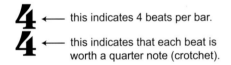

this indicates 4 beats per bar.

this indicates that each beat is worth a quarter note (crotchet).

The time signature indicates the number of beats per bar (the top number) and the type of note receiving one beat (the bottom number). For example:

Thus in $\frac{4}{4}$ time there must be the equivalent of 4 quarter note beats per bar, e.g.

$\frac{4}{4}$ is the most common time signature and is sometimes represented by this symbol called **common time**.

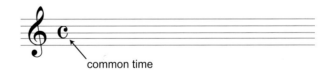

common time

The other time signature used in this book is Three Four Time written $\frac{3}{4}$.
$\frac{3}{4}$ indicates 3 quarter note beats per bar, e.g.

Count, Pick and Fingering Symbols

In the music throughout this book, you will notice symbols representing a metronome (⚗), a pick (♡) and a hand symbol (✋). The metronome symbol (as shown in the above piece) tells you what to count for the particular example. The pick shows you the pick motion and the hand represents left hand fingering.

Chord Diagrams

Chords are learnt with the help of a **chord diagram**. This will show you exactly where to place your left hand fingers in order to play a particular chord. A chord diagram is a grid of horizontal and vertical lines representing the strings and frets of the guitar as shown below.

Chord Symbol ⟶ **C**

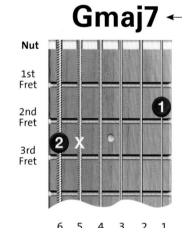

The 6th string is the thickest

The 1st string is the thinnest

Left Hand Fingering

1 Index Finger

3 Ring Finger

2 Middle Finger

4 Little Finger

The **coloured dots** show you where to place your left hand fingers. There are three basic types of chords- **major** (shown as red dots), **minor** (purple dots) and **dominant** (green dots). The **white number** tells you which finger to place on the string just before the fret. If there is no dot on a string, you play it as an open (not fretted) string. The other chord diagram symbols used in this book are summarized with the following two chord shapes.

Dm7 ⟵ Chord symbol for D minor seventh chord.

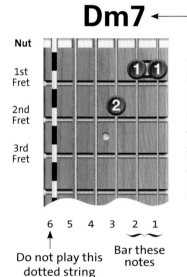

Do not play this dotted string

Bar these notes

A **dotted** string indicates that string is not to be strummed. A small **bar** connecting two black dots indicates they are held down by the same finger. This is called **barring**.

Gmaj7 ⟵ Chord symbol for G major seventh chord.

Dampen this string with the **second finger** by lightly touching it.

An **X** on the string indicates that string is to **dampened** by another finger lightly touching it. The string is still strummed as a part of the chord but it is not heard.

Rhythm Symbols

This is a **half note strum**. It lasts for **two** beats. There are **two** half note strums in one bar of 4/4 time.

These are a pair of **eighth note strums**. Each strum lasts for **half a beat**. There are **eight** eighth note strums in one bar of 4/4 time. Play the larger downward strum louder.

This is a group of three **eighth note triplet strums**. Each strum in the group lasts for **one third** of a beat. There are **twelve** eighth note triplet strums in one bar of 4/4 time. Play the larger downward strum louder.

This is a **quarter note strum**. It lasts for **one** beat. There are **four** quarter note strums in one bar of 4/4 time.

These Strums are a group of **sixteenth note strums**. Each strum lasts for **one quarter** of a beat. There are **sixteen** sixteenth note strums in one bar of 4/4 time. Play the larger downward strum louder.

A broken strum symbol indicates that the strings are not to be strummed.

LESSON ONE

First String Notes

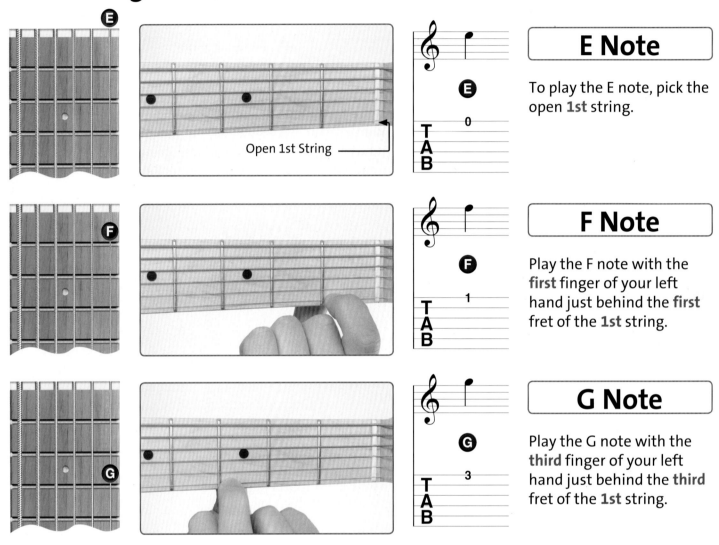

E Note

To play the E note, pick the open **1st** string.

F Note

Play the F note with the **first** finger of your left hand just behind the **first** fret of the **1st** string.

G Note

Play the G note with the **third** finger of your left hand just behind the **third** fret of the **1st** string.

Place your fingers **on their tips**, immediately **behind** the frets and **press** hard to avoid buzzing or deadened notes.

The following examples use **quarter notes** (or crotchets) ♩, worth one count each **(see page 17)**.

Use a **downward** pick motion V. This will apply to all examples and songs until otherwise instructed.

▶ 2.0

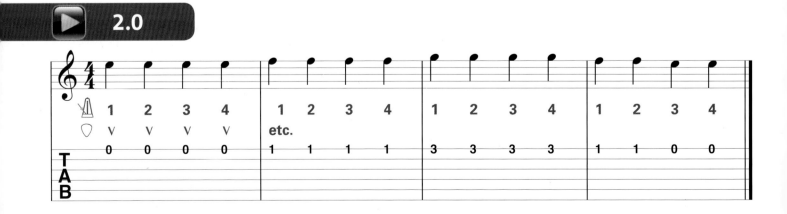

2.1

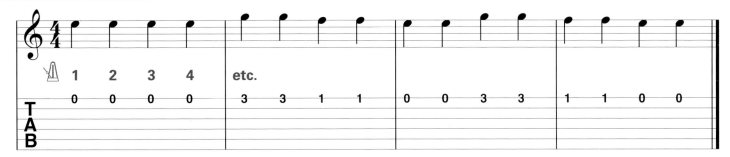

 2.2

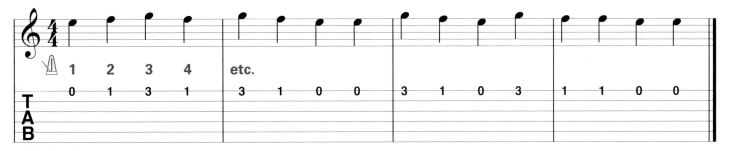

Right Hand Support

It is necessary for the right hand to be supported on the guitar by either (1) the palm resting against the bridge or (2) resting fingers on the pick guard. This will feel more comfortable and aid in the development of speed by encouraging a down/up movement rather than an in/out movement of the pick.

(1) Palm support on bridge

(2) Finger support on pick guard

Pick Technique

You should not let the pick 'dig in' to the strings, but rather play using only its tip.

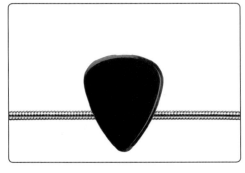

INCORRECT

CORRECT

Trouble-shooting

•Play **slowly** and **evenly. Do not** attempt to go fast as accuracy is more important at this level.
•Place your fingers directly **behind** the frets (**as shown in the photos**) and **on their tips.**
•**Count** (in groups of four) in your head or out loud as you play.
•Be sure to support your wrist and use correct pick technique.

LESSON TWO

Second String Notes

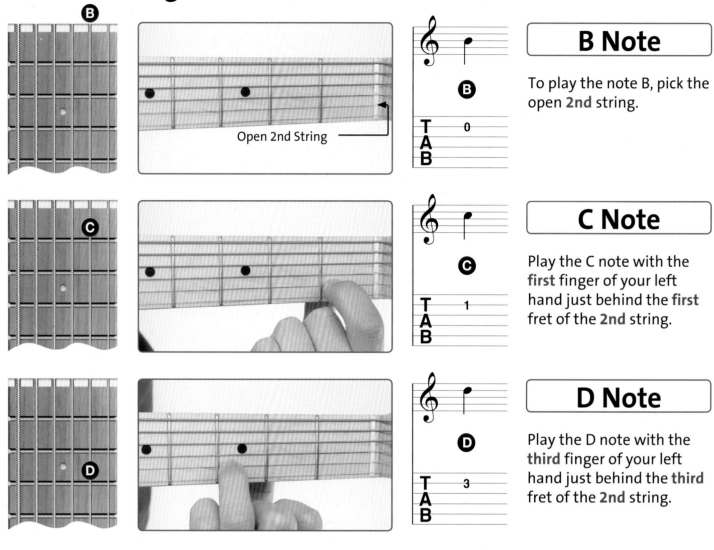

B Note

To play the note B, pick the open **2nd** string.

C Note

Play the C note with the **first** finger of your left hand just behind the **first** fret of the **2nd** string.

D Note

Play the D note with the **third** finger of your left hand just behind the **third** fret of the **2nd** string.

Ex. 3.0 introduces the **half note** (or minim) ♩, which is worth two counts. In bar 8 the half notes are played on the first and third beats, as indicated by the count. This exercise is 8 bars long. Also note the small bar numbers written below the staff.

▶ 3.0

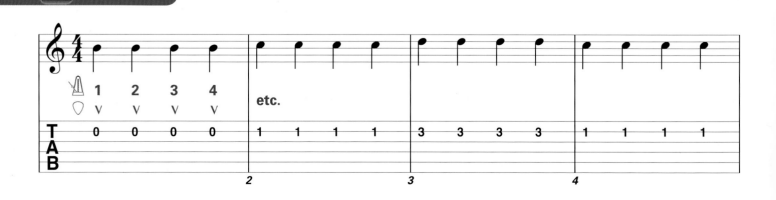

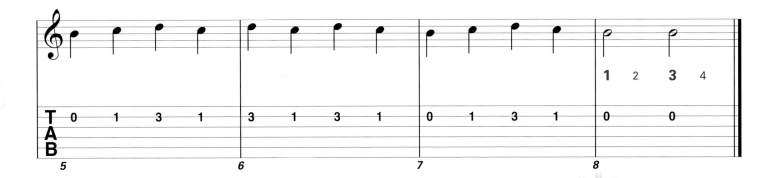

Troubleshooting

*   Make sure your guitar is in tune (**see Appendix One, page 164**).
*   **Watch the music**, not your fingers.
*   Concentrate on learning the notes, rather than memorising the song.
    To do this, you should play very slowly, naming each note as you play it.
*   Remember to use the correct fingering:
    first finger for **first** fret notes, and **third** finger for **third** fret notes.

The following songs make use of all six notes that you have learned so far.

 3.1   Song of Joy (Part One)

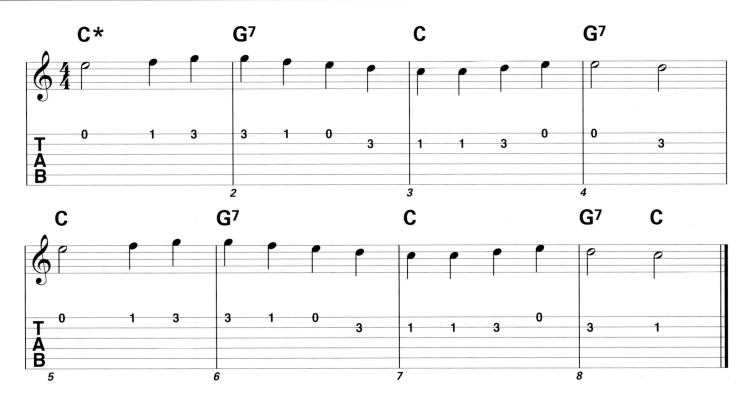

* **Chord symbols** have been included for students who have some chord knowledge.
   You will learn about chords in the following lesson. Chord symbols indicate the chords to be played
   as an accompaniment to the melody.

3.2 **Skip to My Lou**

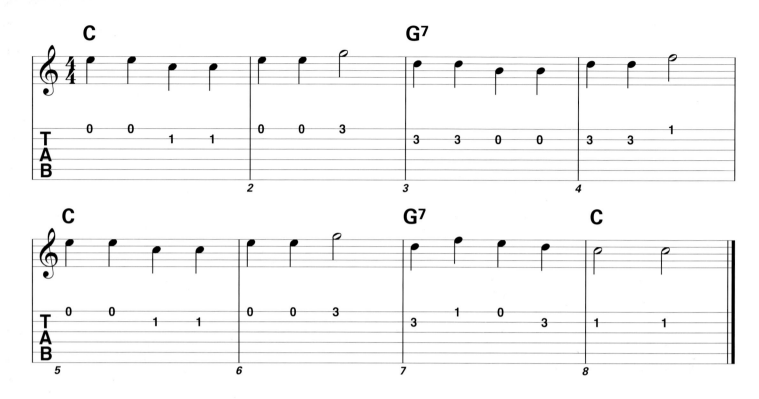

 3.3 **Steps and Skips**

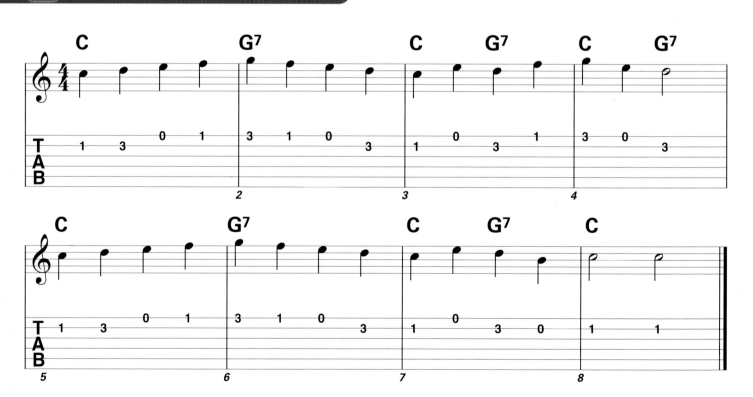

LESSON THREE

Before commencing each lesson or practice session, make sure that your guitar is in tune.
See page 164.

The C Major Chord

A **chord** is a group of three or more notes that are played together. Chords are used to accompany a singer or an instrumentalist who is playing the melody of a song. The first chord you will learn is the **C major chord**, usually just called the **C chord**. Major chords are the most common chords. The C major chord is indicated by the letter **C**. Chords are written on chord diagrams as discussed in the introduction (page 19).

C

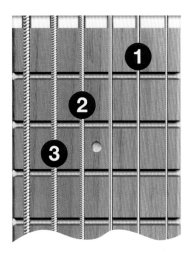

C Major Chord

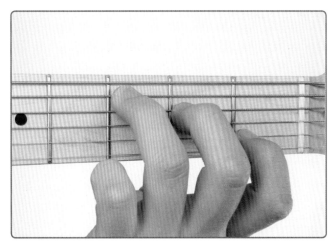

C

To play the **C** chord, place the **first** finger of your left hand just behind the **first** fret of the **second** string, the **second** finger just behind the **second** fret of the **fourth** string and your **third** finger just behind the **third** fret of the **fifth** string.

To play the C chord, play **all six** strings with the pick at the same time using a **downward** motion. This is called a **strum.** Hold the pick lightly and strum from the wrist. Keep your wrist relaxed. If any notes buzz or sound deadened you may have to press harder with the left hand fingers and make sure that your fingers are just behind the fret (not too far back).

Strumming

This is the symbol for a downward strum. This is a **quarter note strum**. It lasts for **one beat**. There are **four** quarter note strums in one bar of $\frac{4}{4}$ time.

This is a **whole note strum**. It lasts for **four beats**. There is **one** whole note strum in one bar of $\frac{4}{4}$ time.

In the following example there are four bars of the **C major** chord played in $\frac{4}{4}$ time. The chord symbol is written above the staff and a new chord symbol is placed at the beginning of each bar. Play the chord with four quarter note strums in each bar. To make the example sound finished always end with one strum of the first chord (a whole note strum ▽).

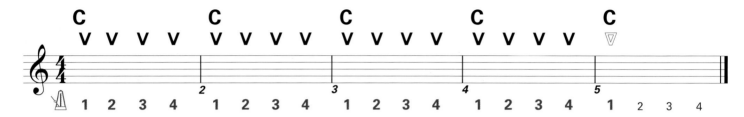

To help keep time play the first quarter note strum in each bar louder.

The Seventh Chord

Another type of common chord is called the **dominant seventh** chord. It is usually referred to as the "**seventh**" chord. The chord symbol for the seventh chord is the number **7** written after the alphabetical letter. The symbol for the **D seventh** chord is **D7**.

D7

D Seventh Chord

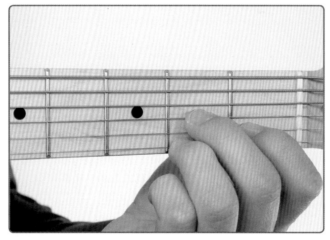

D7

To play the **D7** chord, use the first **three** fingers of your left hand as shown in the diagram, but strum only **five** strings. Do not strum the **6th** string (as indicated by the dotted line).

The Half Note Strum

This is a **half note strum**.

It lasts for **two** beats.

There are **two** half note strums in one bar of $\frac{4}{4}$ time.

In the example below there are four bars of the **D7** chord. Play the **D7** chord with two half note strums in each bar. The **bold** numbers tell you to strum the chord, the **smaller** numbers indicate to hold it until the next strum.

Chord Progressions

Now try using both the **C** and **D7** chords. This is a **chord progression.**

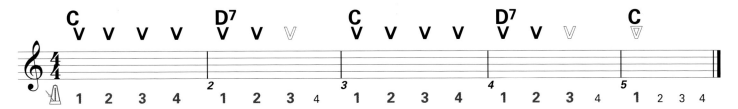

Pivot Finger

When changing between the **C** and **D7** chords, do not move your first finger, as it is common to both chords. The first finger acts as a **pivot** around which the other fingers move. This will make the chord changes easier. Practice slowly and evenly and count or tap your foot as you play to help you keep time.

There are four beats in each bar. When strumming, only your wrist should move. Do not move your arm and keep your forearm resting on the upper edge of the guitar. Remember to keep your left hand fingers just behind the fret. If you place it on top of the fret, the note will sound deadened. If you place it too far back from the fret, the note will buzz and you will have to press down harder to prevent it. If you have an acoustic guitar, pick the string over the sound hole as this results in the best sound.

G7

G Seventh Chord

G7

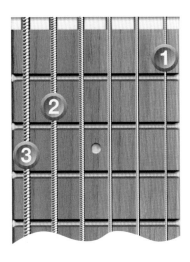

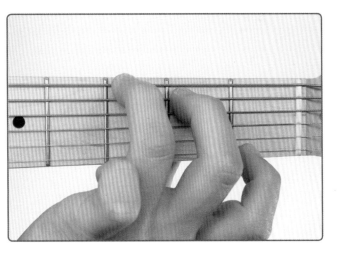

To play the **G7** chord, place the **first, second** and **third** fingers of your left hand as shown in the diagram. Strum all **six** strings.

5.1

The following chord progression contains all three chords you have learnt so far. Use the pivot finger when changing between C and D7.

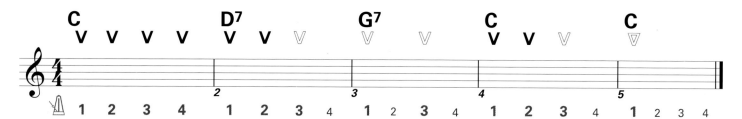

5.2

This chord progression contains two chords in each bar. Each chord receives two beats.

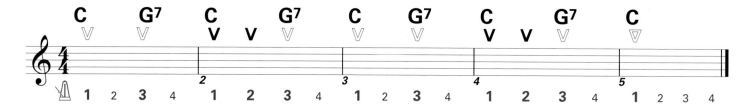

Rhythm Patterns

Instead of changing the strumming for each bar it is quite common to play the same pattern of strums throughout a chord progression. This is called a **rhythm pattern**. It is placed above the staff and indicates the strumming pattern to be played in each bar of music.

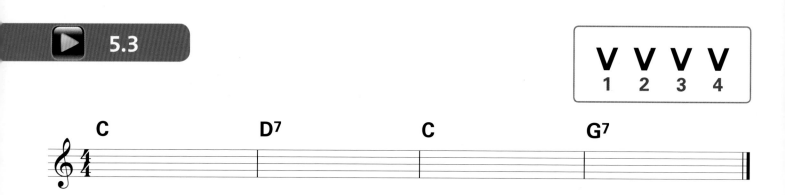
5.3

Open Chord Shapes

The chord shapes given in this lesson and throughout the remainder of the book are called **open chords** because they contain open strings (i.e. no finger is placed on the fret). Another type of chord to learn is called a bar chord. These are commonly used in Rock and Pop music. To learn about bar chords see *Progressive Guitar Method: Bar Chords.*

LESSON FOUR

12 Bar Blues

12 Bar Blues is a pattern of chords which repeats every 12 bars. There are hundreds of well known songs based on this chord progression, i.e. they contain basically the same chords in the same order.
12 bar Blues is common in many styles of music including Blues, Rock, Jazz, Country, Soul and Funk.
Some well known songs which use this 12 bar chord pattern are:

Original Batman TV Theme	Barbara Ann - The Beach Boys
Hound Dog - Elvis Presley	Johnny B Goode - Chuck Berry
Rock Around the Clock - Bill Haley	Dizzy Miss Lizzy - The Beatles
Roll Over Beethoven - Chuck Berry	Red House - Jimi Hendrix
Blue Suede Shoes - Elvis Presley	The Jack - ACDC
In the Mood - Glenn Miller	Ice Cream Man - Van Halen

 6   12 Bar Blues in the Key of G

The following 12 bar Blues is in the **key of G major** and uses all of the chords you have learnt so far.

This pattern of chords will probably sound familiar to you.
Instead of writing a chord symbol above each bar of music, it is common to write a symbol only when the chord changes e.g. the first four bars of this Blues are all **G7** chords. Once you can play this 12 bar Blues, use the chords to accompany **2 String Blues** on the following page.

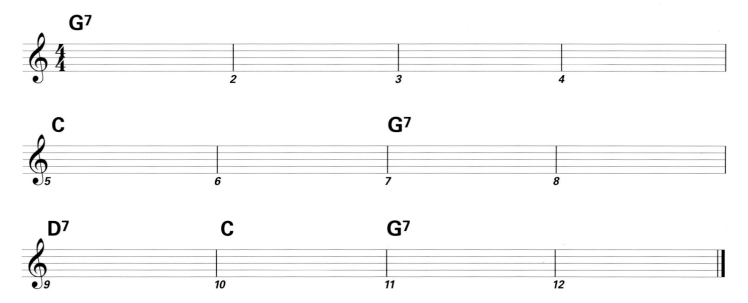

The Whole Note

This is a **whole note**.
It lasts for **four** beats.
There is **one** whole note in one bar of $\frac{4}{4}$ time.

2 String Blues introduces the **whole note (or semibreve)** in bar 12. It is worth four counts.
It is played on the first beat, and held for the remaining three, as indicated by the count.

> ▶ 7 **2 String Blues**

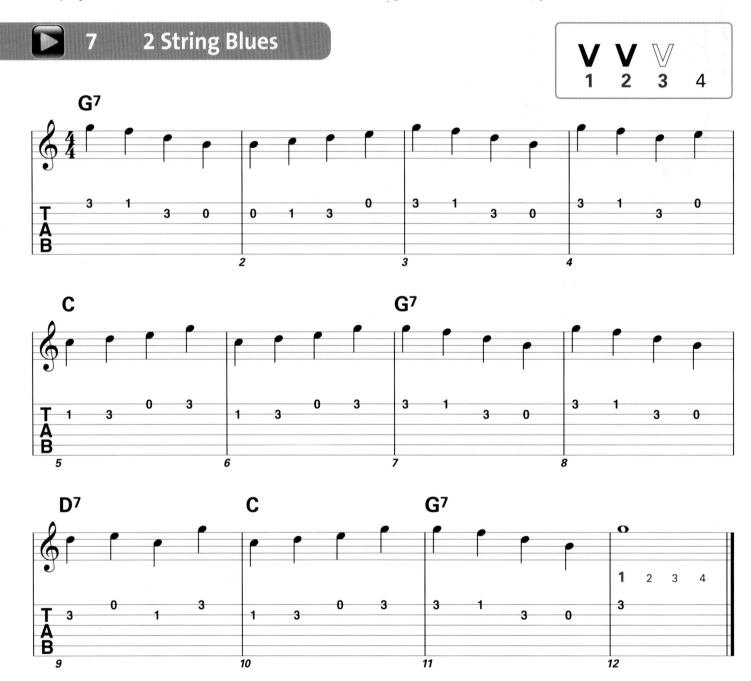

www.learntoplaymusic.com

LESSON FIVE

Third String Notes

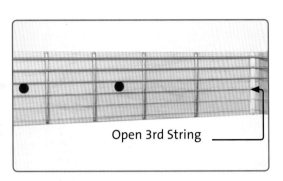

Open 3rd String

G Note

To play the note **G**, pick the open **3rd** string (no fingers placed behind the frets).

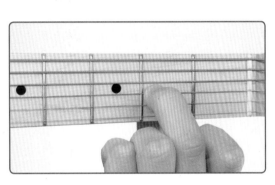

A Note

To play the note **A**, place the **second** finger of your left hand just behind the **second** fret of the **3rd** string.

 8.0

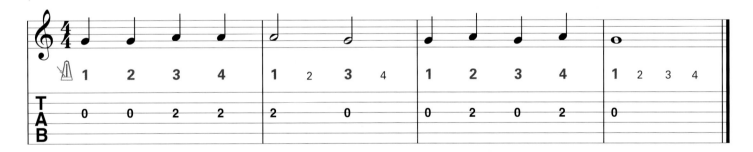

The Octave

You now have two **G** notes; the one shown above and the one at the third fret on the first string.
This type of repetition occurs with all notes, since the musical alphabet goes from **A** to **G**, and then back
to **A** again. The distance between the two **G** notes is called an **octave**.

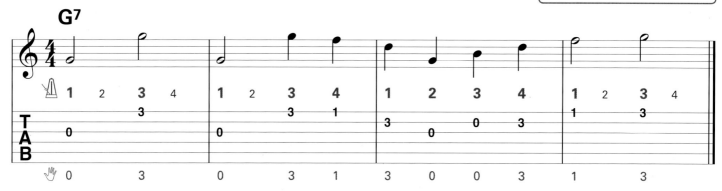

G Major Chord

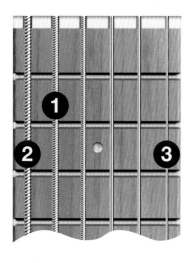

G

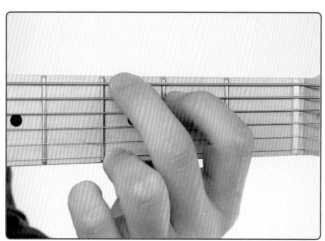

To play the **G** chord, place the **first**, **second** and **third** fingers of your left hand as shown in the diagram. Strum all **six** strings.

Slide Finger

9.0   Changing from G to D7

The following example contains the **G** and **D7** chords.
When changing from **G** to **D7**, do not lift your third finger off the string, but slide it down to the second fret. Only touch the string very lightly as you do this.
When changing from **D7** to **G**, slide your third finger up to the third fret.

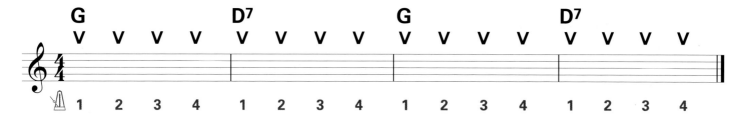

Here are some songs to practice your chord changes with.
These melodies contain all the notes you have learnt so far.

9.1   Cycling in G

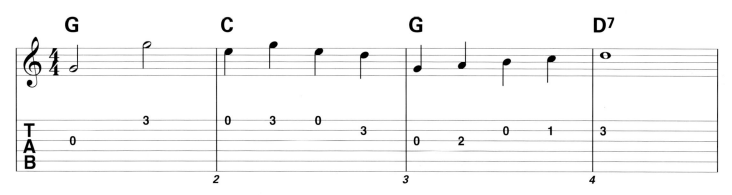

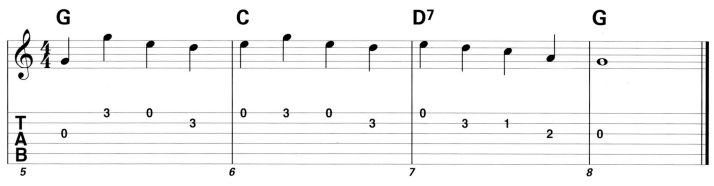

Accessories…
Acoustic Guitar Pickups

Fingerpicking is mostly played on acoustic guitars. If you are playing in public, at some point you will need to amplify your guitar.

The most common way of doing this is to get a pickup fitted to your guitar and plug it into either an acoustic guitar amp, or the PA system used by the singer. There are many pickups available for acoustic guitars and most can be attached for a performance and then removed until required again.

9.2   Three String Blues

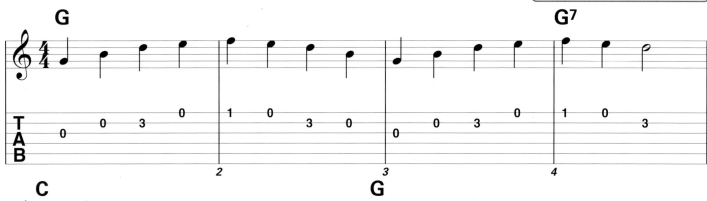

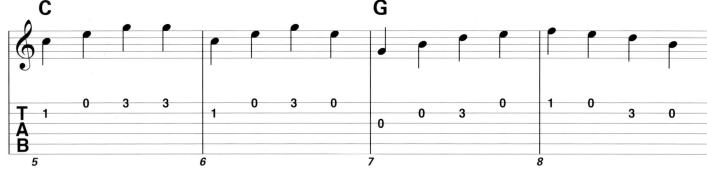

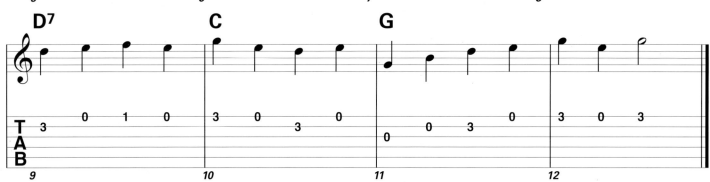

9.3   Guitar Boogie

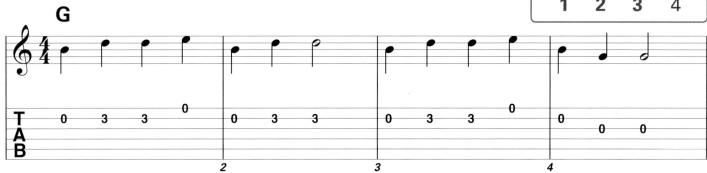

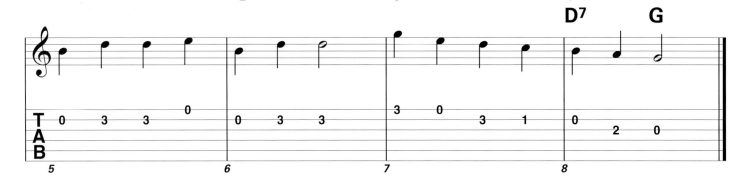

LESSON SIX

Eighth Note Rhythms

All the rhythm patterns you have played so far involved playing a downward strum (**V**) on the 1st, 2nd, 3rd or 4th beat. To make rhythm patterns more interesting, **eighth note rhythm** patterns can be used. An eighth note rhythm is a combination of a down and an up strum within one beat. The down strum "on the beat" is played louder than the up strum which is "off the beat" (the "+" section of the count). An **up strum** is indicated by a **∧**, and is played on the "**and**" section of the count. Start the up strum on the first (thinnest) string and strum all six strings.

Play the following rhythm pattern, which has eighth note strums on the second beat consisting of a down strum on the "2" count and an up strum on the "+" section of the count. There are **eight** eighth note strums in one bar of $\frac{4}{4}$ time.

 10   **Eighth Note Rhythm Pattern 1**

V V∧V V
1 2 + 3 4

Practice this new rhythm pattern holding a **G** chord then apply it to the chord progression below.

G   C   G   D⁷

 11

11.1
V∧V V V
1 + 2 3 4

11.2
V V V V∧
1 2 3 4 +

11.3
V V V∧V
1 2 3 + 4

11.4
V∧V∧V∧V∧
1 + 2 + 3 + 4 +

11.5
V∧V∧V V
1 + 2 + 3 4

11.6
V V∧V V∧
1 2 + 3 4 +

11.7
V∧V∧V∧V
1 + 2 + 3 + 4

11.8
V V∧V∧V
1 2 + 3 + 4

12.0   12 Bar Blues

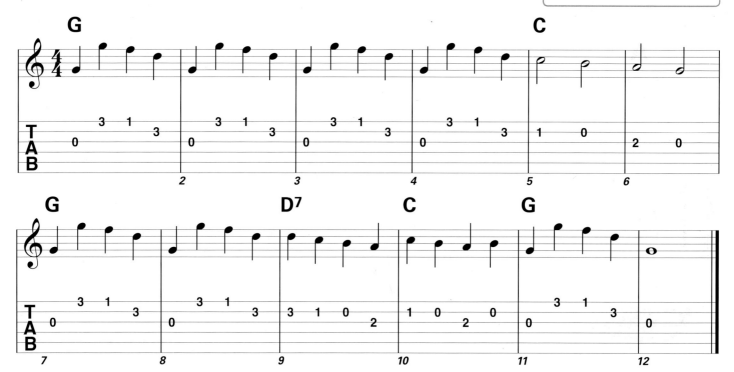

The Lead-In

This song introduces **lead-in notes**, which are notes occurring before the first complete bar of music. These notes should be played on counts three and four of a count-in (as indicated). You will notice that the final bar of the song contains only one half note (two counts), which acts as a "balance" to the lead-in notes. This is quite common, but does not always occur. Lead-in notes are sometimes called pick up notes.

12.1   Michael Row the Boat Ashore

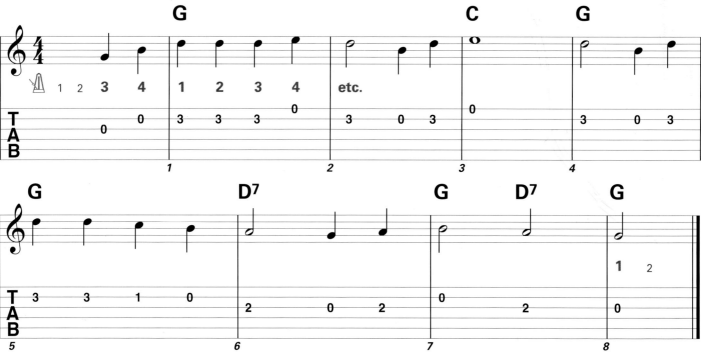

A Major Chord

A

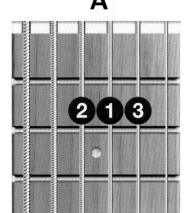

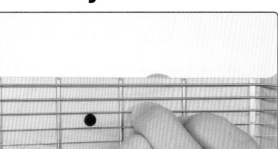

When changing between **C** and **A** use your second finger as a pivot.

A

To play the **A** chord, place the **first**, **second** and **third** fingers of your left hand as shown in the diagram. Strum all **six** strings.

C	A	D⁷	G⁷

$\frac{4}{4}$

E Major Chord

E

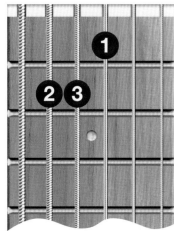

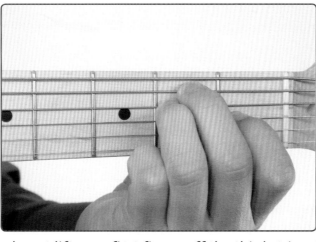

E

To play the **E** chord, place the **first**, **second** and **third** fingers of your left hand as shown in the diagram. Strum all **six** strings.

When changing from **E** to **A**, do not lift your first finger off the third string, but slide it down to the second fret. Only touch the third string very lightly as you do this. The use of the slide will make changing between **E** and **A** chords easier. Then play the following chord progression using the two bar rhythm pattern as shown.

First Bar   Second Bar

E	A	E	A

$\frac{4}{4}$

The following chord progression uses the same two bar rhythm pattern as in the previous example, but contains two chords, each receiving two beats, in bars 1, 2 and 3.

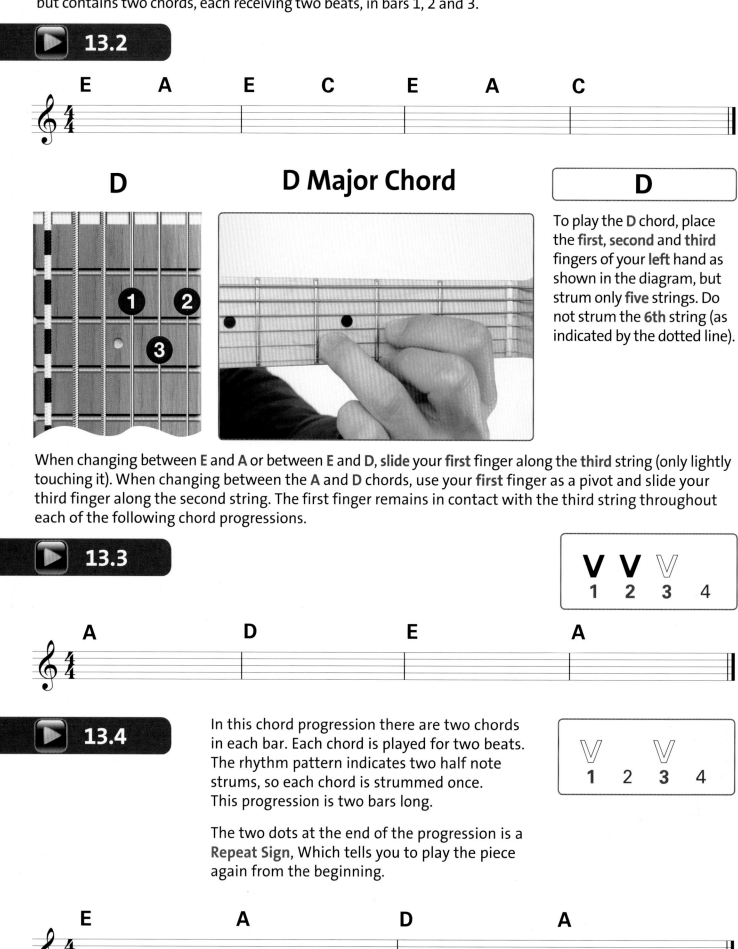

D Major Chord

D

To play the **D** chord, place the **first**, **second** and **third** fingers of your **left** hand as shown in the diagram, but strum only **five** strings. Do not strum the **6th** string (as indicated by the dotted line).

When changing between **E** and **A** or between **E** and **D**, **slide** your **first** finger along the **third** string (only lightly touching it). When changing between the **A** and **D** chords, use your **first** finger as a pivot and slide your third finger along the second string. The first finger remains in contact with the third string throughout each of the following chord progressions.

In this chord progression there are two chords in each bar. Each chord is played for two beats. The rhythm pattern indicates two half note strums, so each chord is strummed once. This progression is two bars long.

The two dots at the end of the progression is a **Repeat Sign**, Which tells you to play the piece again from the beginning.

Repeat sign

LESSON EIGHT

12 Bar Blues and Seventh Chords

12 bar blues (and most chord progressions) can be played in any key. The following 12 bar Blues is in the **key of A major**. When a song is said to be in the key of **A major**, it means that the most important chord (and usually the first chord) is the **A** chord.

 14   **12 Bar Blues in the Key of A Major**

V V∧V∧V
1 2 + 3 + 4

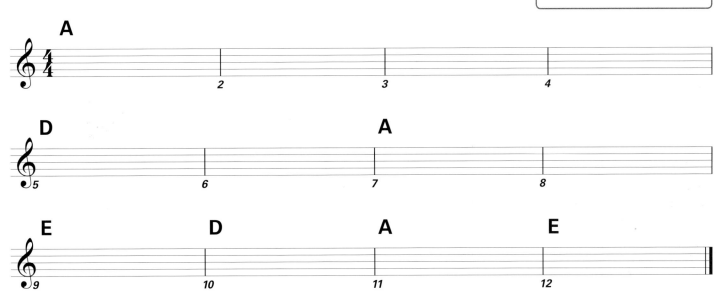

E7

E Seventh Chord

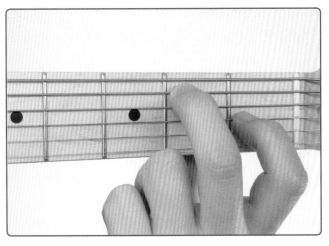

E7

To play the **E7** chord, use the **first** and **second** fingers of your left hand as shown in the diagram, and strum all **six** strings. The **E7** chord shape is just the **E** chord shape with the **third** finger lifted off.

The next chord progression contains an **E7** chord and uses the eighth note rhythm pattern shown above (introduced in exercise 10 on page 35). When changing between **D** and **E7** use your **first** finger as a **slide** finger. When changing between **A** and **D** use your **first** finger as a **pivot**.

A Seventh Chord

A7

 A7

To play the **A7** chord, use the **second** and **third** fingers of your left hand as shown in the diagram, and strum all **six** strings. The **A7** chord shape is just an **A** chord shape with the **first** finger lifted off.

This progression contains an **A7** chord and uses the eighth note rhythm pattern shown above (introduced in exercise 11.1 on page 35). When changing between **D7** and **G** use your **third** finger as a slide finger.

Here is a 12 bar Blues melody to be accompanied by the new chords you have learnt.

Guitar Effects...
Chorus Pedal

The chorus pedal is an ambient effect which creates a feeling of space and movement within the sound. The pedal delays the sound and changes it to become less regular and also adds slight pitch fluctuations. It then mixes this version of the sound in with the original signal coming from the guitar. Chorus pedals are equally effective with both acoustic and electric guitars.

A **repeat sign** in the final bar indicates that the song must be played again from the beginning. Repeat signs can also be used at the end of a section.
In this song the repeat sign at the end of bar 4 indicates a repeat of the first four bars.

Note Summary

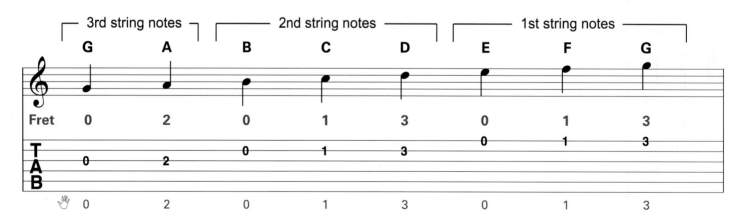

LESSON NINE

Minor Chords

There are three main types of chords: **Major**, **Seventh** and **Minor**. The chord symbol for the **minor** chord is a small '**m**' placed after the letter name. Here are some commonly used open minor chord shapes.

Dm

D Minor Chord

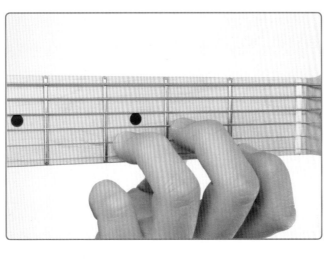

Dm

To play the **Dm** chord, use the **first**, **second** and **third** fingers of your left hand as shown in the diagram. Strum only **five** strings.

 17.0

In this progression use a **pivot** finger when changing from **C** to **A7** and **Dm** to **G7**. Use a **slide** finger between **A7** and **Dm**.

V V∧V∧V
1   2 + 3 + 4

| C | A⁷ | Dm | G⁷ |

Am

A Minor Chord

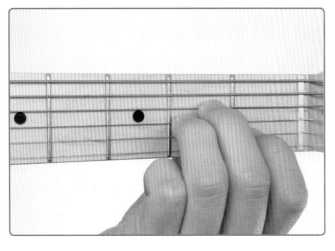

Am

To play the **Am** chord, use the **first**, **second** and **third** fingers of your left hand as shown in the diagram. Strum all **six** strings.

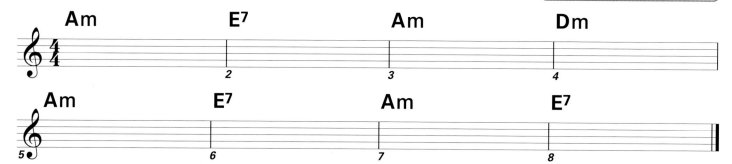

The Three Four Time Signature

This is the **three four time signature**. It indicates that there are **three** beats in each bar. Three four time is also known as waltz time. There are three quarter notes in one bar of $\frac{3}{4}$ time.

The following chord progression is written in $\frac{3}{4}$ time. To help keep time, accent (play louder) the first strum in each bar. Use your **first** and **second** fingers as **pivots** when changing between **C** and **Am**. Use your **first** finger as a **pivot** when changing between **Dm** and **G7**.

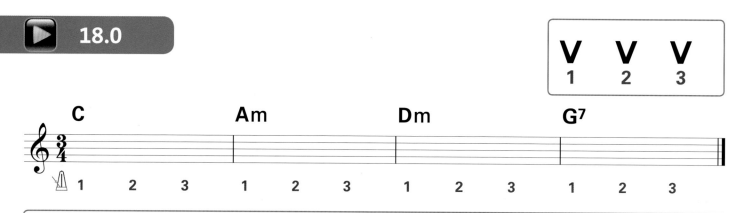

Guitar Effects…
The Pod

The Line 6 Pod is a portable amp simulator for guitar. You can plug any electric guitar into it and by changing the settings, you can emulate the sound of the guitar being played through many different amps. The sounds range from Traditional Fender and Vox amps to Marshall stacks, through to high gain modern Mesa Boogie amps.

¾ Time Rhythm Patterns

Practice the following ¾ time rhythm patterns holding a **C** chord shape.
Apply any of these patterns to the above chord progression.

▶ 18.1-18.6

18.1

V		V	∧	V
1		2	+	3

18.2

V	∧	V		V
1	+	2		3

18.3

V		V		V	∧
1		2		3	+

18.4

V	∧	V	∧	V
1	+	2	+	3

18.5

V		V	∧	V	∧
1		2	+	3	+

18.6

V	∧	V	∧	V	∧
1	+	2	+	3	+

Em

E Minor Chord

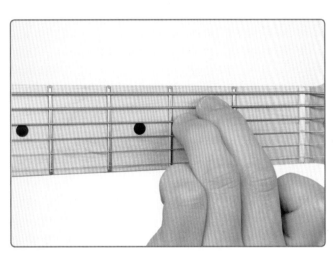

Em

To play the **Em** chord, use the **second** and **third** fingers of your left hand as shown in the diagram. Strum all **six** strings. The **Em** chord shape is just the **E** chord shape with the **first** finger lifted off.

The following chord progression is in ¾ time and uses the three minor chords introduced. Use your **first** finger as a **pivot** when changing between **Dm** and **G7**. Use your **second** finger as a **pivot** when changing between **G7** and **Em**.

▶ 18.7

V		V	∧	V		V		V		V
1		2	+	3		1		2		3

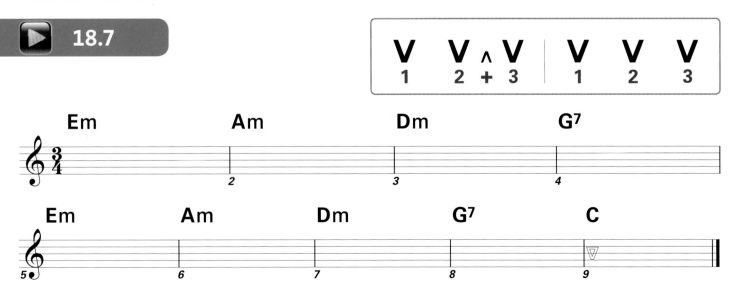

Bass Note Rhythm Pattern

Bass notes are the notes on the 6th, 5th and 4th strings. Instead of strumming the complete chord for every beat, try picking the bass note of the chord on the first beat and then strum the first three or four strings of the chord on the 2nd and 3rd beats. Play the following bass note rhythm holding a **G** chord shape.

 19.0

The best bass note to pick is the lowest note of the chord that has the same letter name of the chord. This is called the root note.

When playing a **G** chord, pick the 6th string note (**G** note).
When playing an **Em** chord, pick the 6th string note (**E** note).
When playing an **Am** chord, pick the 5th string note (**A** note).
When playing a **D7** chord, pick the 4th string note (**D** note).

Practice this rhythm technique on each chord separately at first, and remember to hold the full chord shape even though you are not playing all the strings.

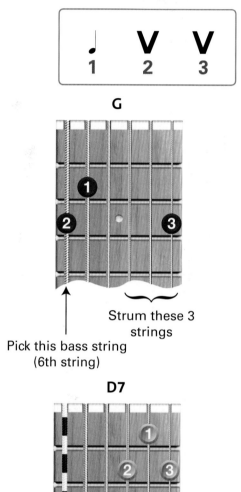

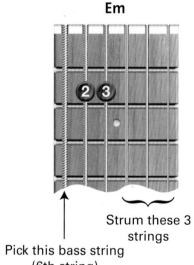
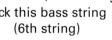

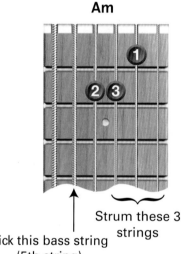
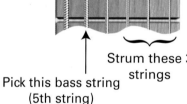

 19.1

Play this chord progression using the bass note rhythm pattern.

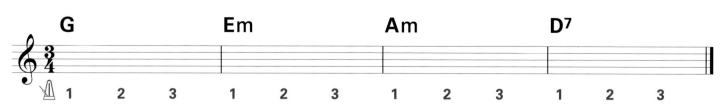

LESSON TEN

Fourth String Notes

 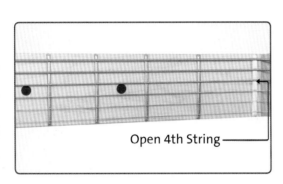 

D Note

To play the **D** note, pick the open **4th** string.

 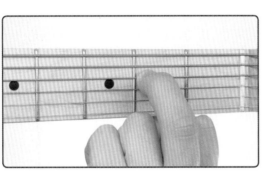 

E Note

Play the **E** note with the **second** finger of your left hand behind the **second** fret of the **4th** string.

 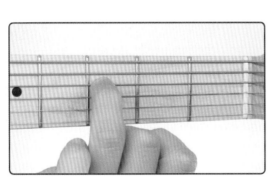 

F Note

Play the **F** note with the **third** finger of your left hand behind the **third** fret of the **4th** string.

The Dotted Half Note

The Dotted Half Strum

A dot placed after a note or strum extends its value by **half**. A dot placed after a half note or half note strum means that you hold it for three beats. One dotted half note makes one bar of music in $\frac{3}{4}$ time. There is one dotted half note strum in one bar of music in $\frac{3}{4}$ time. Use a dotted half strum to play the chords which accompany the following melody.

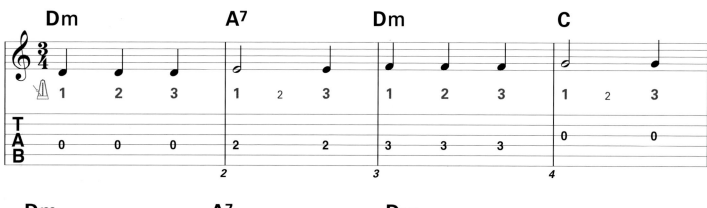

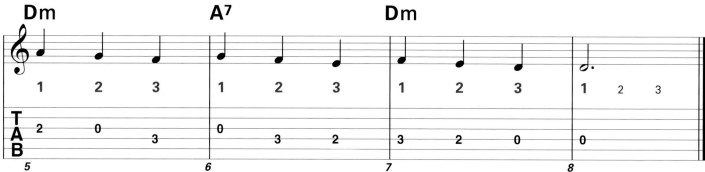

 20.1   Molly Malone

Use the bass note rhythm pattern shown adjacent to accompany this song.
Play the first **G** bass note where the **G** chord symbol is written above the first bar, rather than where
the lead-in note occurs. Once you can play both the melody and accompaniment to a song, try playing
one part while your teacher or another guitarist plays the other part. Then you can swap parts when
the song repeats. This will prepare you for playing both rhythm and lead guitar.

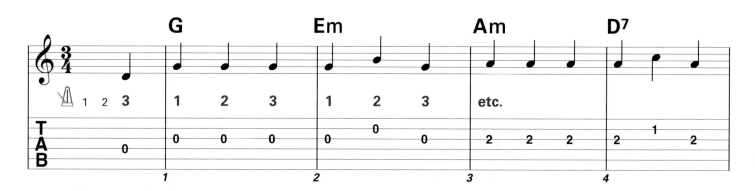

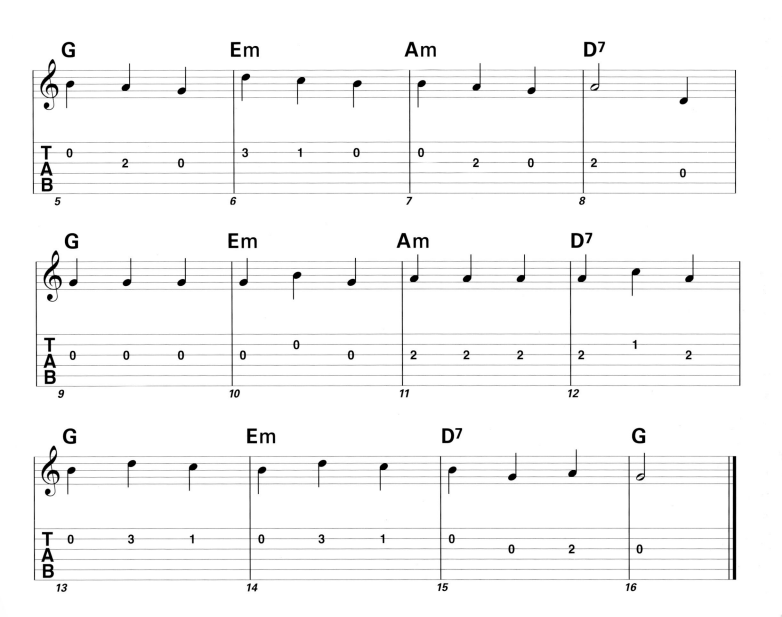

Know your Guitars...
The Classical Guitar

The classical guitar has nylon strings and is played with the fingers of the right hand rather than a pick. As the name suggests, this is the type of guitar used for classical music, but it is also commonly used for Flamenco, Folk, and World music. Some of the most famous classical guitarists are Andres Segovia, John Williams and Alirio Diaz. American fingerpicker Chet Atkins used an electric classical guitar.

The Tie

A **tie** is a curved line joining two or more notes of the same pitch. The second note (or notes) is **not played**, but its time value is added to that of the first note. In bar 1 the **G** note is held for a total of 4 counts (2+2) and in bar 15 it is held for 6 counts (4+2).

21.0   Will the Circle Be Unbroken

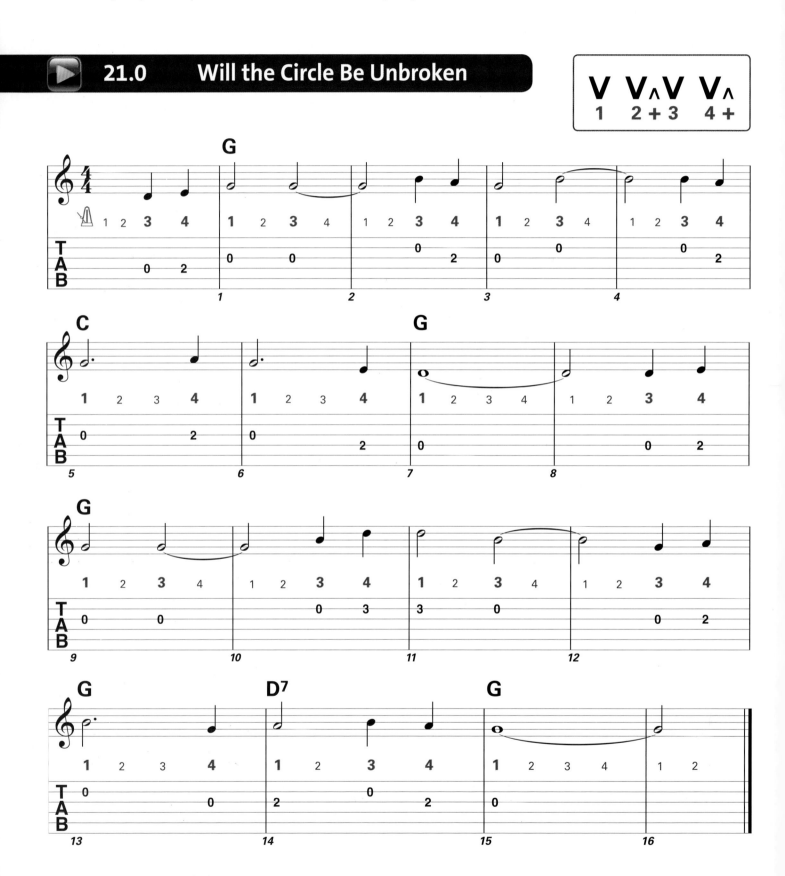

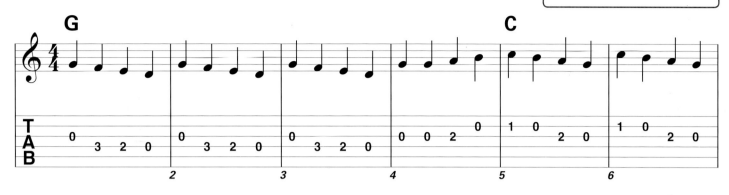

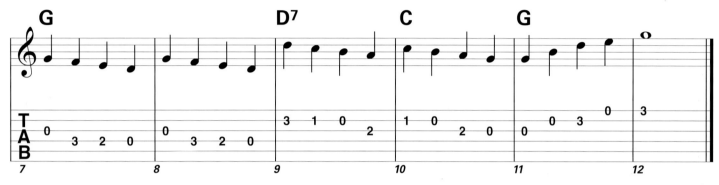

Note Summary

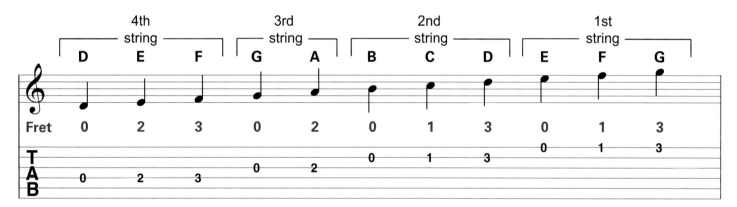

Troubleshooting

- Remember to maintain correct left and right hand playing positions (**see photos on page 15**).
- **Count** out loud as you play, and be particularly careful of dotted notes and ties.
  It may also help to tap your foot with the beat.
- Hold the pick correctly, between the thumb and index finger (**see page 14**).
- Be sure to support your wrist and use correct pick technique (**see page 21**).

LESSON ELEVEN

Fifth String Notes

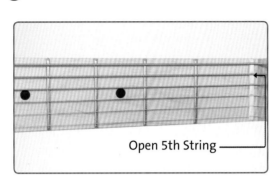

Open 5th String

A Note

To play the A note, pick the open **5th** string.

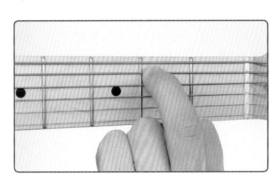

B Note

Play the B note with the **second** finger of your left hand behind the **second** fret of the **5th** string.

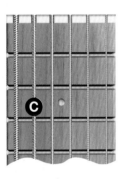
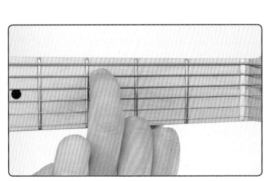

C Note

Play the C note with the **third** finger of your left hand behind the **third** fret of the **5th** string.

 22.0   Volga Boatman

V V∧V V∧
1 2 + 3 4 +

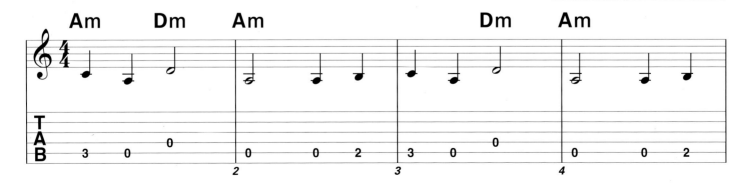

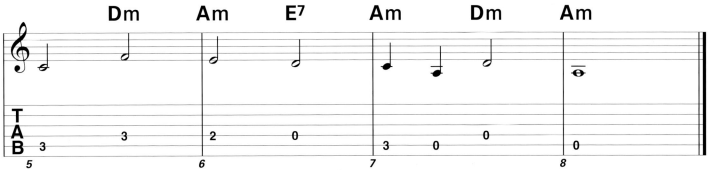

22.1   Blow the Man Down

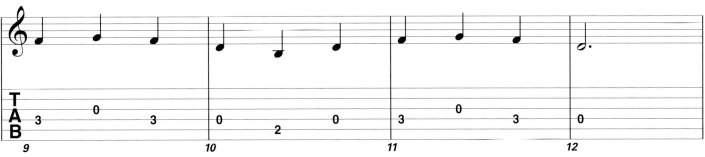

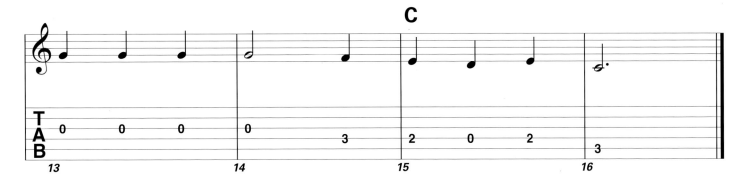

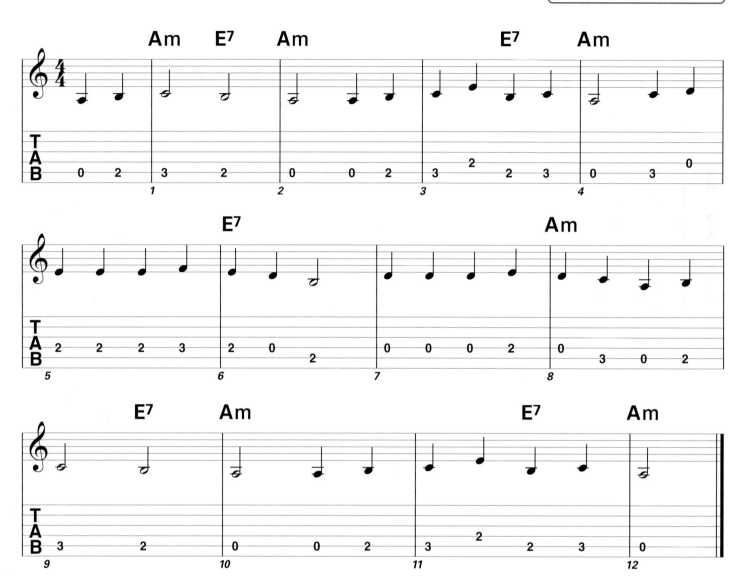

Note Summary

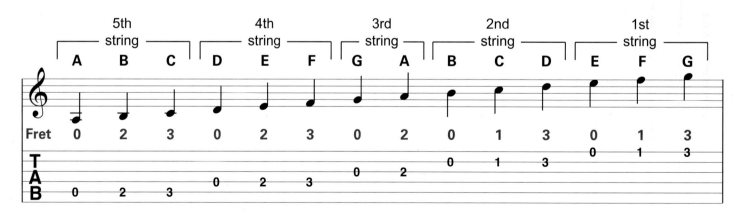

LESSON TWELVE

F

F Major Chord

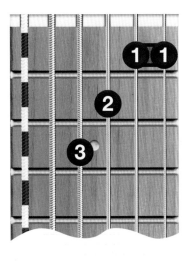

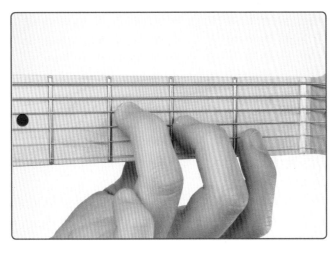

To play the **F** chord, use the **first**, **second** and **third** fingers of your left hand as shown in the diagram. Strum only **five** strings. The **first** finger **bars** across the first two strings. This is quite difficult at first. The **F** chord is easier to play if you position your **third** and **second** before positioning the first finger.

 23.0

$$V \wedge V \wedge V \wedge V$$
$$1 + 2 + 3 + 4$$

Remember that you can use any rhythm pattern you like on any chord progression as long as they have the same time signature e.g. $\frac{4}{4}$ time.

C   Em   F   G⁷

C7

C Seventh Chord

C7

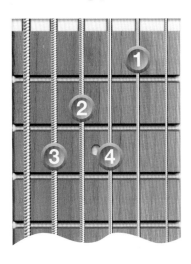

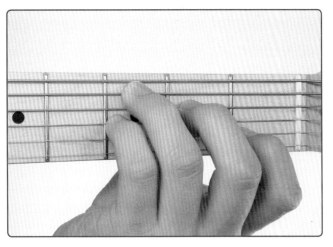

To play the **C7** chord, use the **four** fingers of your left hand as shown in the diagram, and strum all **six** strings. The **C7** chord is a **C** chord with an added **B♭** note played by the fourth finger.

23.1

Use your **second** finger as a **pivot** when changing between the **F** and **Dm chords**. Use your **first** and **second** fingers as **pivots** when changing between **Am** and **C7**.

F	Dm	Am	C7

Turnaround Progressions

In Lesson Four, you were introduced to the 12 bar Blues chord progression. Another important chord progression is the **turnaround**. Like 12 bar Blues, it is the basis of many songs, and it will probably sound familiar to you also. The first chord progression on the previous page is a turnaround in the key of **C major**.

Unlike 12 bar Blues, where the progression occurs over a fixed number of bars, the turnaround progression may vary in length as in the examples below. However, the **chord sequence** remains the same. Some of the biggest hit records of all time are based upon a turnaround progression. Every year since the beginning of Rock there have been hit songs based upon 12 bar Blues or turnarounds.

Some songs that are based upon a turnaround progression are:

Stand by Me - John Lennon
I Will Always Love You - Whitney Housten
Return to Sender - Elvis Presley
All I Have to do is Dream - The Everly Brothers
Crocodile Rock - Elton John
Everlasting Love - U2

Houses of the Holy - Led Zeppelin
Uptown Girl - Billy Joel
Blue Moon - various artists
Tell Me Why - The Beatles
Hungry Heart - Bruce Springsteen

 24.0 **Turnaround Progression in the Key of G Major**

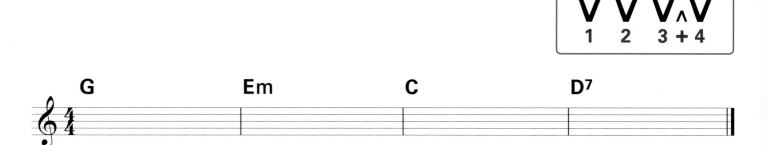

G	Em	C	D7

Alternative Chord Fingerings

To make the chord changes in the previous progression easier, play the **Em** chord with your **first** and **second** fingers. This will allow the use of **pivot** fingers between **G** to **Em** and **Em** to **C**. A pivot can also be used between **C** and **D7** and a **slide** finger between **G** and **D7**. Alternative fingering for any chord shape can be used to make chord progressions easier to play.

 24.1   Turnaround Progression in the Key of C Major

In this turnaround there are two chords in each bar.
Use your **first** and **second** fingers as **pivots** when changing between **C** and **Am**.

| C | Am | F | G⁷ | C | Am | F | G⁷ |

Notice the similarity in sound between the previous two Turnaround progressions.
They are the **same** progression but in two different keys.

Guitar Effects...
Delay Pedal

The delay pedal makes a copy of what a guitarist plays and repeats it at a specific rate depending on how the controls are set. You can control the speed of the delay and the number of repeats. Delays are used to great effect by Edge from U2, David Gilmour of Pink Floyd and Andy Summers of the Police.

Rests

In music, rests are used to indicate periods of silence. For each note value there is a corresponding rest, as outlined in the following table.

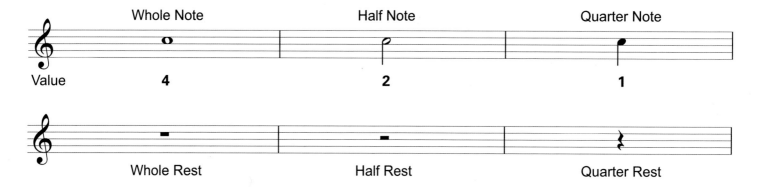

The Common Time Signature

The **C** at the beginning of this exercise stands for **common time**, which is another name for $\frac{4}{4}$ time.

25.0

V V∧V V∧
1 2 + 3 4 +

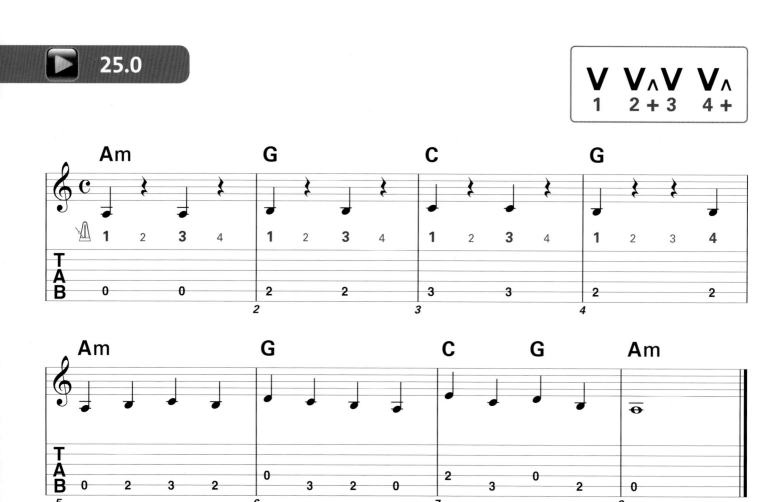

25.1   Banks of the Ohio

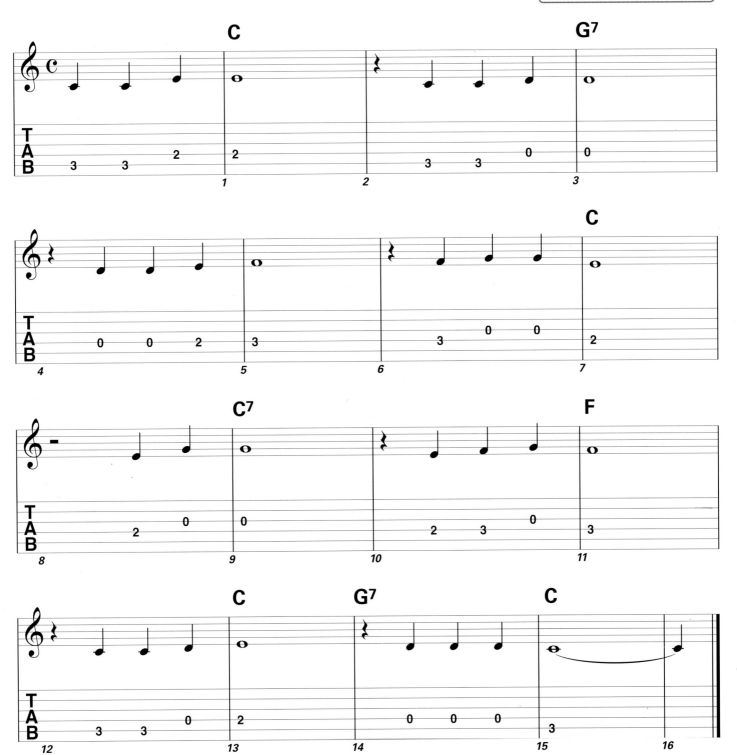

LESSON FOURTEEN

Sixth String Notes

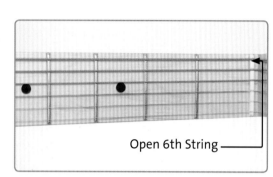

Open 6th String

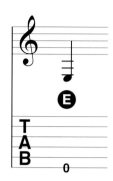

E Note

To play the E note, pick the open **6th** string.

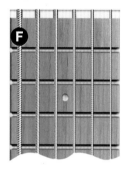

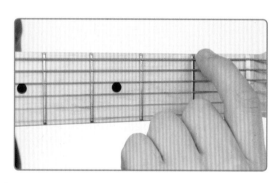

F Note

Play the F note with the **first** finger of your left hand behind the **first** fret of the **6th** string.

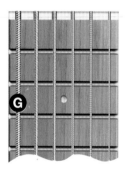

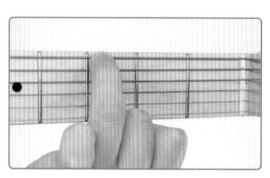

G Note

Play the G note with the **third** finger of your left hand behind the **third** fret of the **6th** string.

 26.0

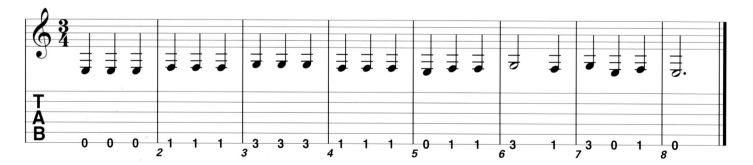

www.learntoplaymusic.com

Know your Guitars...
Dobro

The Dobro is a metal bodied "Resonator Guitar". It has a resonator cone which amplifies the sound even though there are no electronics involved. There are also wooden bodied guitars with a metal resonator cone. All these guitars are great for slide and fingerpicking. They are traditionally associated with Blues, Bluegrass, Country and other Roots music.

26.2 **12 Bar Blues in the Key of C**

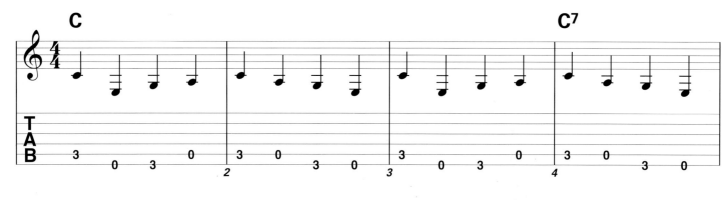

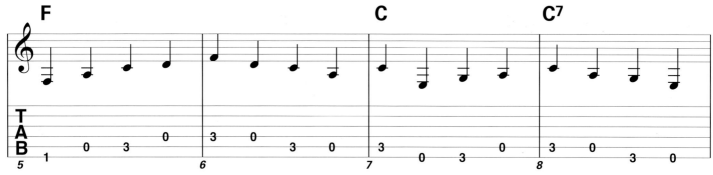

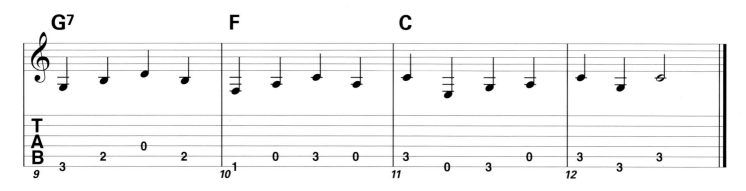

27 **Asturias**

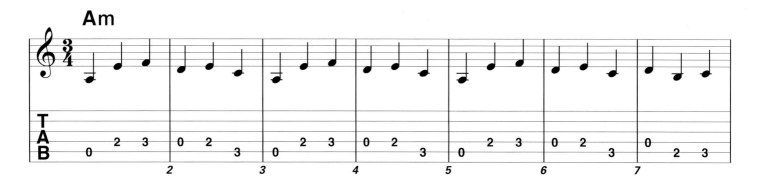

Know your Guitars…
Fender Stratocaster

The Fender Stratocaster is one of the most famous of all electric guitars. Designed by Leo Fender and first released in 1954, the Stratocaster (commonly called a "Strat") has been used by millions of guitarists all over the world. Some of the most famous Strat players include Jimi Hendrix, Mark Knopfler and Eric Clapton.

Open Position Notes

All of the notes you have studied, as summarised below, are in the **open position**.
The open position consists of the open string notes and the notes on the first three frets.

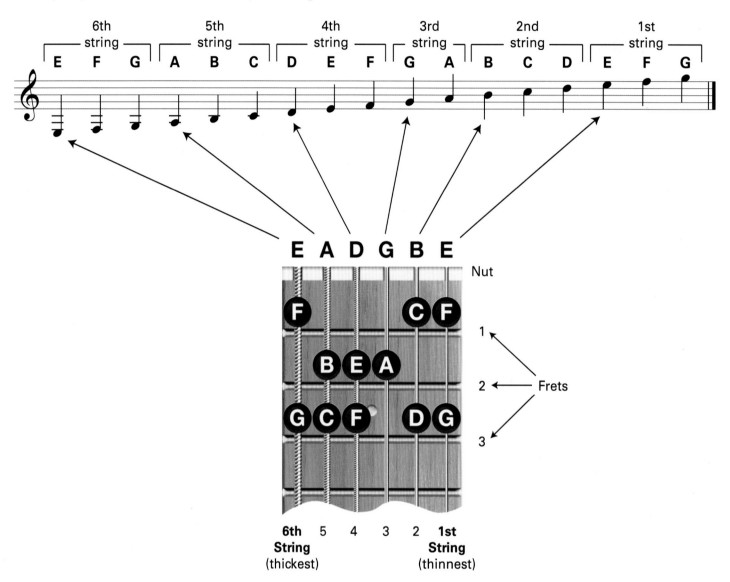

By playing through the notes you will notice **B** to **C** and **E** to **F** are only one fret apart (called a **semitone**), whereas all other notes are two frets apart (called a **tone**). The distance between notes of the musical alphabet can be set out as such:

semitones (i.e. one fret apart)

It is essential for you to remember this pattern of notes.

Troubleshooting
- Revise all songs and exercises so far studied.
- Double-check your timing and smoothness of sound. To do this, try recording yourself.
- Remember to watch the music, **not** the guitar.

LESSON FIFTEEN

Eighth Notes

An **eighth note (or quaver)** ♪ is worth half a count. Two eighth notes, which are usually joined by a line (called a beam) ♫, have the same value as a quarter note.

Eighth notes are counted as such:

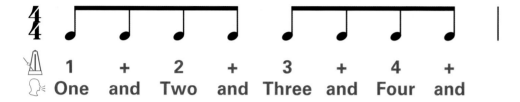

Here is a combination of half notes, quarter notes and eighth notes in ¾ time.

The **eighth note rest** ⅞, is worth half a count of silence.

Alternate Picking

All of the melodies you have played so far involved a downward pick motion, indicated by V. With the introduction of eighth notes, the technique of down and up (∧) picking is used. This is called **alternate picking**, and it is essential for the development of speed and accuracy.

In alternate picking, use a down pick **on** the beat (the number count) and an up pick **off** the beat (the 'and' count). Try the following exercise:

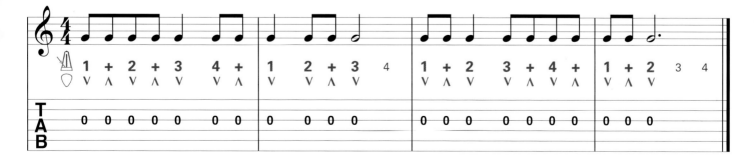

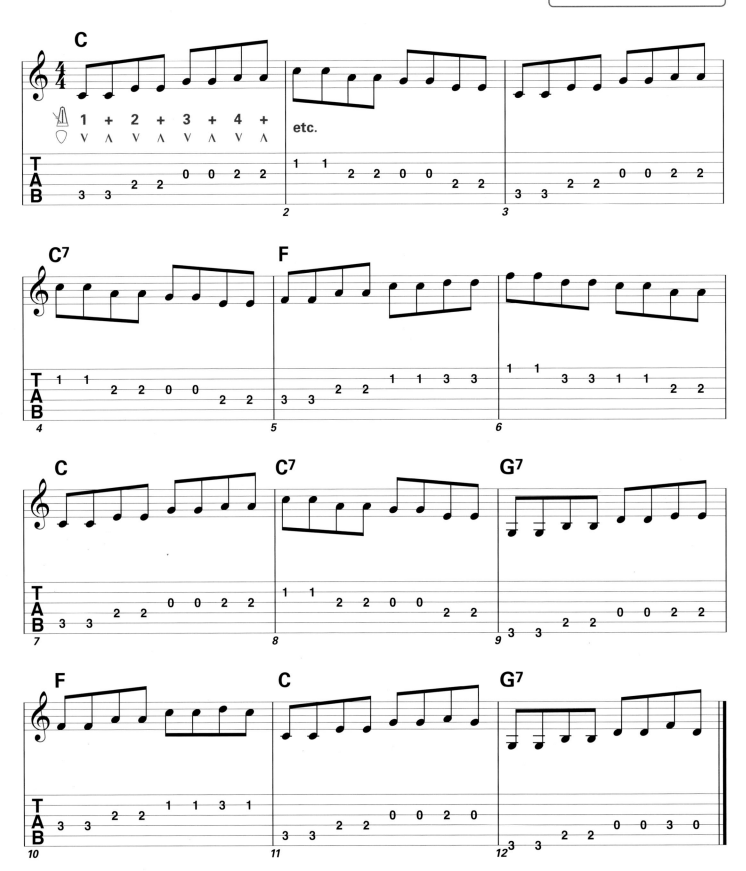

www.learntoplaymusic.com

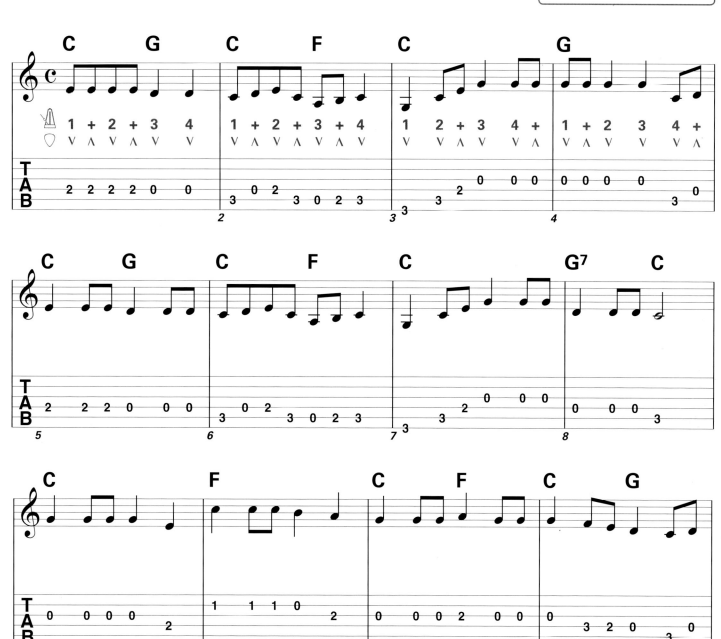

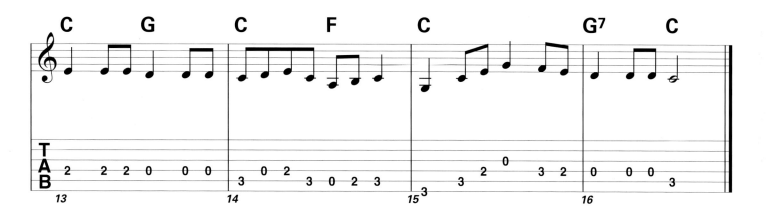

Duets

It is important for you to be able to play with other musicians and the best practice for this is the study of duets. Duets are written as two independent parts of music, which are indicated by the Roman Numerals at the beginning of each line. In classical music the first guitar is called Primo ($\bar{I}$) and second guitar Secondo ($\bar{II}$).
To get the most benefit from duets practice **both** parts.

Playing duets will present specific problems.
Be careful of the following:

- Make sure to stay on your correct part
  (e.g. either the top or bottom line).
- Pay particular attention to your timing and try not
  to stop if the other guitarist makes a mistake.
- Do not be distracted by the other guitarist's part.

30.1   Song of Joy

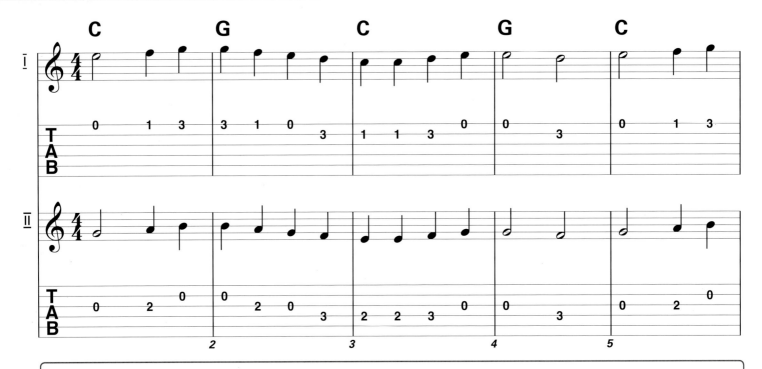

Know your Guitars...
The Fender Telecaster

This classic solid body electric guitar is used extensively in Country music and is also popular with Rock, Pop, Soul, Funk and Blues players. It is capable of producing a variety of sounds from clear bell like tones to stinging attacking sounds. Equally effective for both Rhythm and Lead guitar, the Telecaster has been favored by players like James Burton (who played with Elvis Presley), Muddy Waters, Albert Lee and Roy Buchanan.

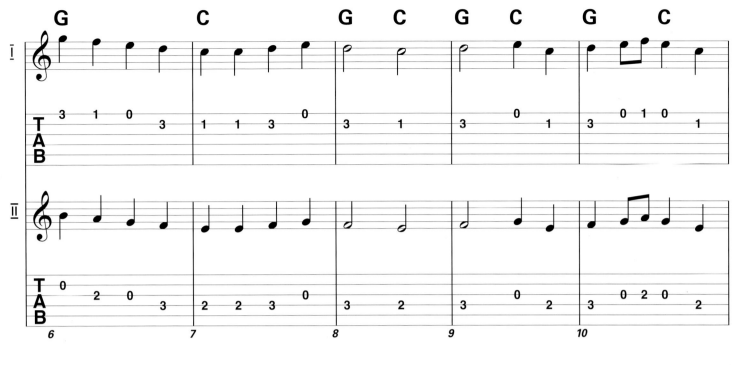

Amplifiers...
The Fender Twin

The most famous of all combo amps is the Fender Twin Reverb. It produces a crisp clean tone, even at high volumes and is used by players of many different musical styles. Many players use a Fender Twin as their basic sound and combine it with pedals to achieve distortion and other effects.

LESSON SIXTEEN

Bm

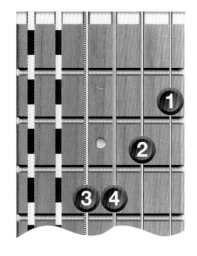

B Minor Chord

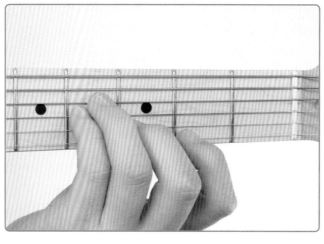

Bm

To play the **Bm** chord, use the **first**, **second**, **third** and **fourth** fingers of your left hand as shown in the diagram. Strum only **four** strings.

The following progression is a turnaround in the key of D major. It contains the **Bm** chord and there are two chords per bar each receiving two counts. Notice that this progression sounds similar to the turnarounds you have already learnt.

▶ **31.0**

| D | Bm | G | A | D | Bm | G | A |

The following turnaround is in the key of **G major**. Each chord is played for two bars.

▶ **31.1**

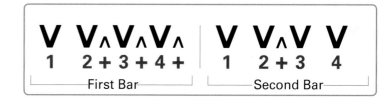

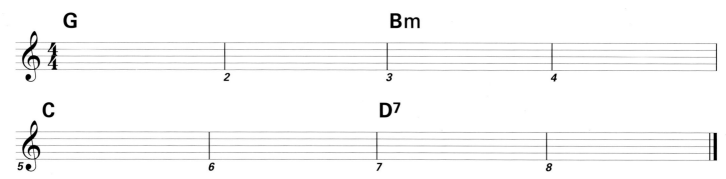

B7

B Seventh Chord

To play the **B7** chord, use all **four** fingers of your left hand as shown in the diagram. Strum only **five** strings.

Some guitarists deaden the 6th string by lightly touching it with the left hand thumb which reaches over the top of the neck. The 6th string can then be strummed but it won't sound as it is deadened. This technique can apply to any chord where the 6th string note is not a part of the chord shape.

| A | B⁷ | D | E⁷ |

| Em | D⁷ | C⁷ | B⁷ |

This progression contains both **B7** and **Bm**.

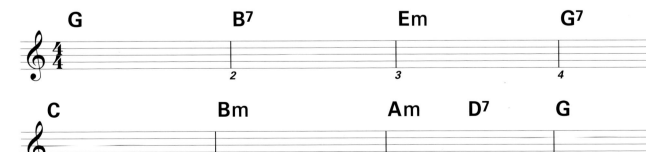

LESSON SEVENTEEN

Sharps

A sharp (♯) is a sign, placed immediately **before** a note, which raises the pitch of that note by **one semitone (one fret)**. When you see a note with a sharp sign in front of it, you should first think of where the normal note is located (in music this is called the **natural** note), and then sharpen it by placing your **next finger** on the **next fret** along. Here are some examples:

2nd String	1st String	3rd String	5th String
2nd Fret	2nd Fret	1st Fret	4th Fret
2nd Finger	2nd Finger	1st Finger	4th Finger

The use of the sharp sign introduces five new notes, occurring in between the seven natural notes which you already know. The following exercise outlines all twelve notes which occur within one octave of music. Play through it **very slowly**, and be sure to use correct fingering for the sharpened notes.

▶ **33.0**

You will notice that there is no sharp between **B** and **C**, or between **E** and **F**.
The exercise you have just played is called a **chromatic scale**. It is referred to as the **A chromatic scale** because the starting and finishing notes are **A** (this is called the **Key note** or **tonic**).
The chromatic scale consists entirely of **semitones** i.e. it moves up (or down) one fret at a time.

▶ **33.1**   Here is the **G** chromatic scale:

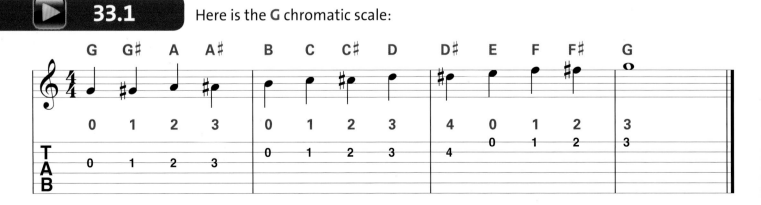

When a note is sharpened it **REMAINS** sharp until either a **BAR LINE** or a **NATURAL SIGN** (♮) cancels it. Check the following notes:

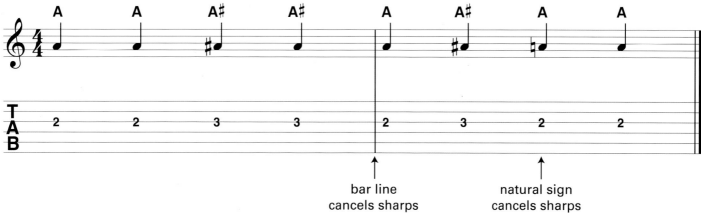

bar line
cancels sharps

natural sign
cancels sharps

34   **House of the Rising Sun**

35   Dark Eyes

Watch your timing with the ties in this song.

36   Minuet

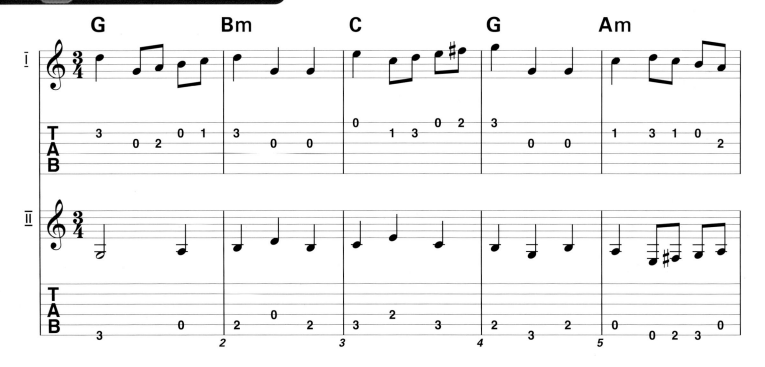

Troubleshooting

- Be sure to use the correct fingering for all notes:

  1st fret .... 1st finger

  2nd fret .... 2nd finger

  3rd fret .... 3rd finger

  4th fret .... 4th finger

- Keep your left hand fingers as close to the strings as possible.
  This will greatly improve your accuracy and speed.

- **Watch** the music and **read** the notes.
  Occasionally you should just name the notes in a song, without actually playing through it.

LESSON EIGHTEEN

Flats

A **flat** (♭) is a sign, placed immediately **before** a note, which **lowers** the pitch of that note by one semitone. Locate the following flats:

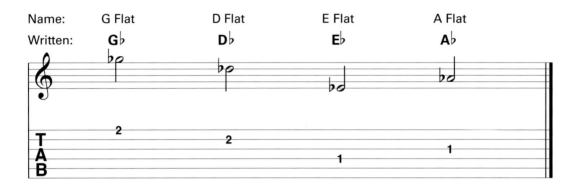

When an open string note is flattened, the new note must be located on the **next lower string** e.g.:

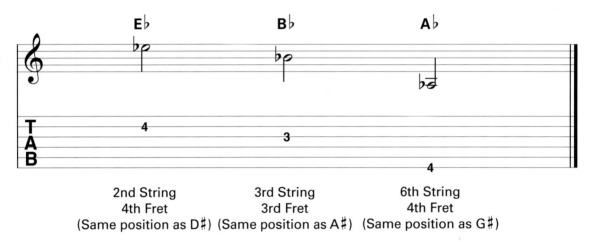

2nd String	3rd String	6th String
4th Fret	3rd Fret	4th Fret
(Same position as D♯)	(Same position as A♯)	(Same position as G♯)

You will notice that it is possible for the same note (in pitch) to have two different names. For example, F♯ = G♭ and G♯ = A♭. These are referred to as **enharmonic** notes. The following fretboard diagram outlines all of the notes in the **first position** on the guitar (including both names for the enharmonic notes). The first position consists of the open string notes and the notes on the first four frets.

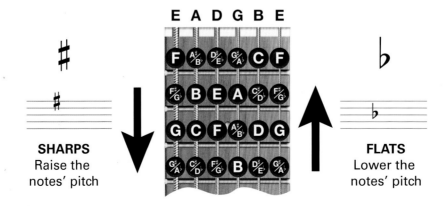

SHARPS
Raise the notes' pitch

FLATS
Lower the notes' pitch

Here are two octaves of the **E chromatic scale**, ascending using sharps and descending using flats.

As with sharps, flats are cancelled by a bar line or by a natural sign.

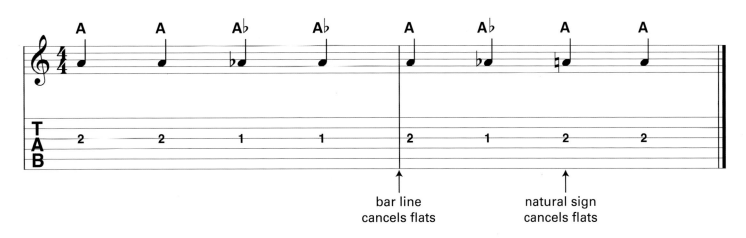

bar line
cancels flats

natural sign
cancels flats

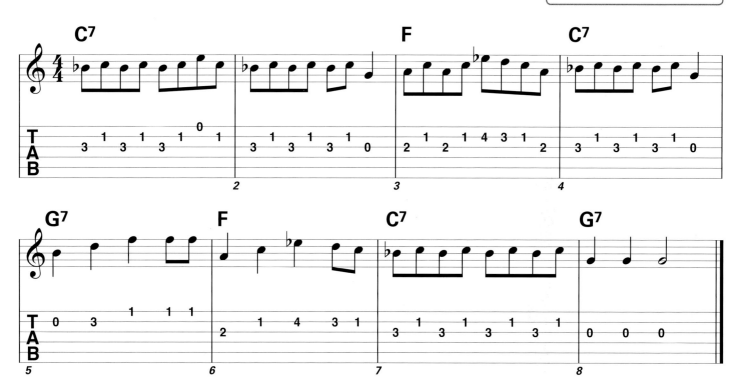

First and Second Endings

This song introduces **first** and **second endings (see Line 6)**. On the first time through, ending **one** is played, as indicated by the bracket:
The section of music is then repeated (go back to the beginning of line 5) and on the second time ending **two** is played. Be careful **not** to play both endings together.

39   **Hall of the Mountain King**

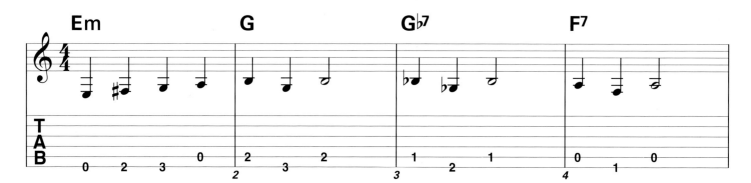

If you are playing the chords to this song it is easier to play the G♭7, F7 and B chords as **bar chords.**
To learn how to play bar chords see Progressive Guitar Method: Bar Chords.

LESSON NINETEEN

Silent Strums and Continuous Rhythm

The basic $\frac{4}{4}$ rhythm pattern learnt in Lesson Three consisted of four down strums, i.e.

$$\begin{array}{cccc} V & V & V & V \\ 1 & 2 & 3 & 4 \end{array}$$

After playing the first strum, your right hand moves upwards in preparation for the second strum. The strings are not played on this upward movement. This upward motion can be represented by a broken upward strum symbol (⋏) which indicates that the strings are not strummed (a silent strum).

So the basic rhythm above could be written as:

$$\begin{array}{cccccccc} V & \wedge & V & \wedge & V & \wedge & V & \wedge \\ 1 & + & 2 & + & 3 & + & 4 & + \end{array}$$

The above two rhythm patterns sound exactly the same.

If you watch your **right** hand you will notice that it actually moves **up and down** in a **continuous motion** but it only makes contact with the strings on the **down** strum.

Also when you play eighth note rhythms you will see that your right hand also moves up and down in a continuous motion sometimes making contact with the string and sometimes not.

Silent Strum Symbols

When an **upward** strum is made without contacting the strings it can be represented by ⋏.

When a **downward** strum is made without contacting the strings it can be represented by ⩔̇ .

Some very useful and interesting rhythm patterns can result by incorporating eighth note rhythms with silent down strums. ⩔̇

 40.0

$$\begin{array}{ccccc} V & V & \wedge & \dot{V} & \wedge & V \\ 1 & 2 & + & 3 & + & 4 \end{array}$$

Try the following rhythm holding a **C** chord.

This rhythm is the same as eighth note rhythm pattern 2 in Lesson Six, except the down strum on the third beat does not make contact with the strings. Practice this rhythm until you perfect it. You can apply it to any chord progression you like. This is a very important rhythm and will be the basis of many other rhythms.
Apply this rhythm pattern to the following chord progression. Use pivot and slide fingers where possible to make the chord changes easier.

Try a variation of this rhythm pattern on the following turnaround progression in the key of G. To make the chord changes easier use the alternative fingerings on page 56.

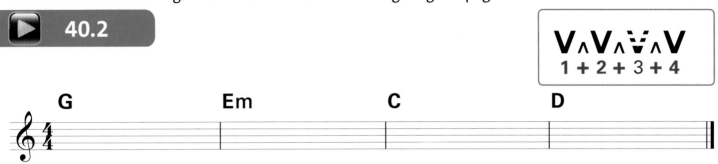

The following variation has a silent **down** strum on the 2nd and 3rd beat. Apply it to the progression below.

When changing between **C** and **A7** use your **second** finger as a pivot.

Rhythm Variations

Try the following rhythm variations and make up your own. Apply these rhythms to any chord progression you like. A **G** chord is used on the recording. All these suggested variations are in $\frac{4}{4}$ time but the same principle can be applied to $\frac{3}{4}$ time. Also note that in all these rhythms your **right** hand moves up and down in a **continuous motion**. These rhythm patterns can sound "off the beat". This is called **syncopation**.

41.0	41.1	41.2
V V ♥∧V 1 2 3 + 4	V∧♥∧V∧V∧ 1 + 2 + 3 + 4 +	V∧V∧♥∧♥∧ 1 + 2 + 3 + 4 +

41.3	41.4	41.5
V∧♥∧♥∧♥∧ 1 + 2 + 3 + 4 +	V∧♥∧♥∧V∧ 1 + 2 + 3 + 4 +	♥∧♥∧♥∧♥∧ 1 + 2 + 3 + 4 +

42 **Blues Traveller**

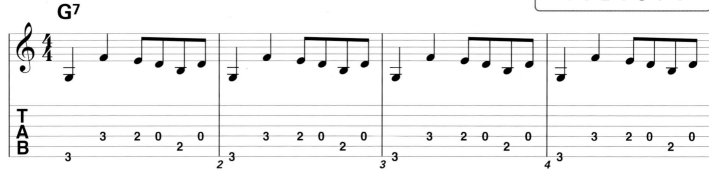

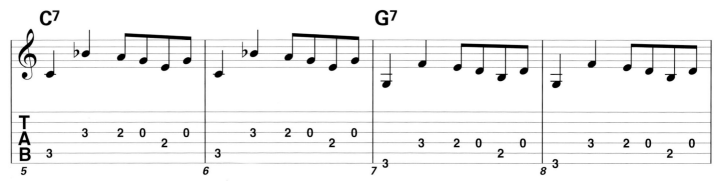

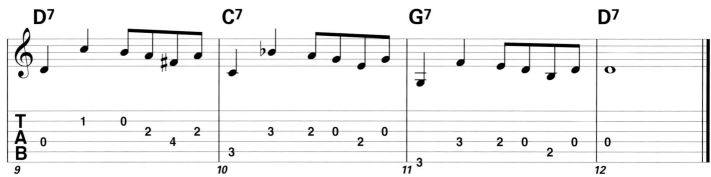

 43 **Blue Seas**

Know your Guitars…

The Flying V

This dramatic looking guitar was first released by Gibson in 1958. Like the Les Paul, it contains two humbucking pickups and is great for playing Rock, Blues and Metal. It was used extensively by Bluesmen Albert King and Lonnie Mack, as well as Jimi Hendrix. A later version released by Jackson was used by Randy Rhoads when he was Ozzy Ozborne's lead guitarist. Today there are many different Flying V style guitars available.

LESSON TWENTY

Dotted Quarter Notes

A **dotted quarter note** is worth 1½ counts. It has the same time value as a quarter note tied to an eighth note, i.e.

When a dotted quarter note is followed by an eighth note, as in Greensleeves, the count is as follows:

44   Greensleeves

This song features some difficult left hand fingering passages which will require special attention. In any music you play, be sure to **isolate** difficult sections and practice them thoroughly.
The eighth notes in Greensleeves are played with an up pick, as indicated.

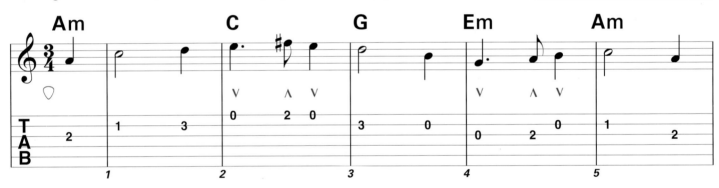

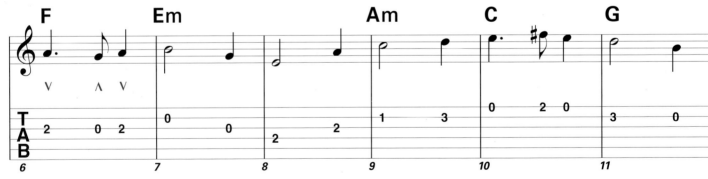

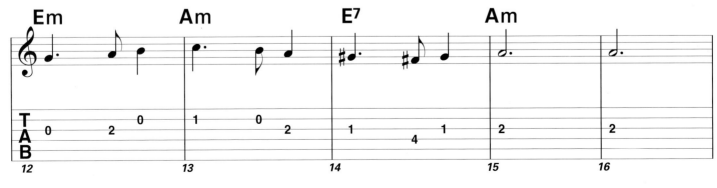

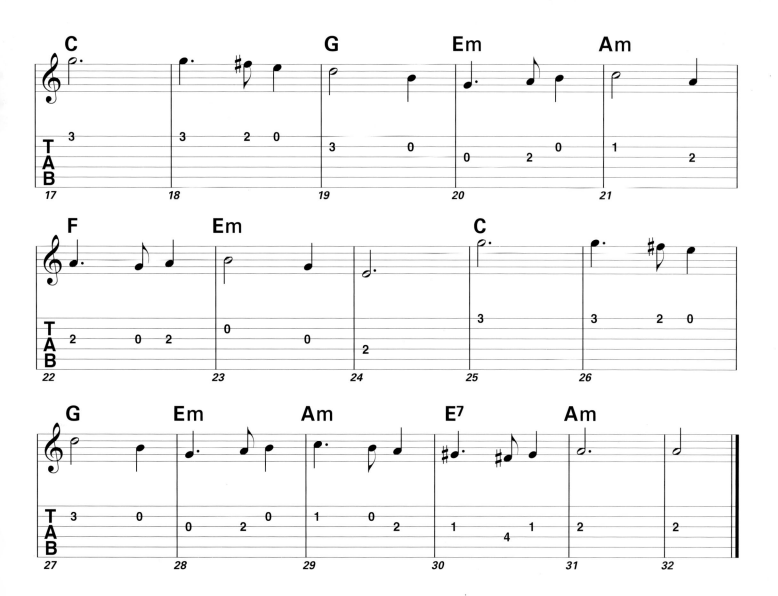

The 'High' A Note

The **'high' A note** is located on the 5th fret of the first string, and is played using the **fourth** finger.

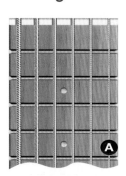

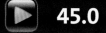

45.0 Practice the following exercise slowly and carefully. Watch the music!

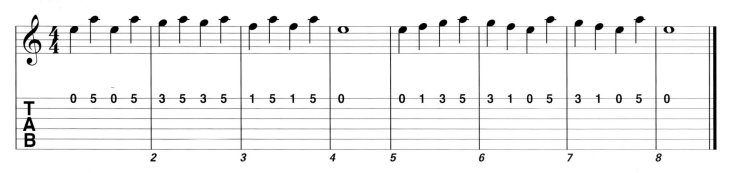

45.1 Scarborough Fair

Scarborough Fair uses the high **A** note in bars 6, 8 and 9. The abbreviation **rit,** in bar 15, stands for **ritardando**, which means to **gradually slow down**.

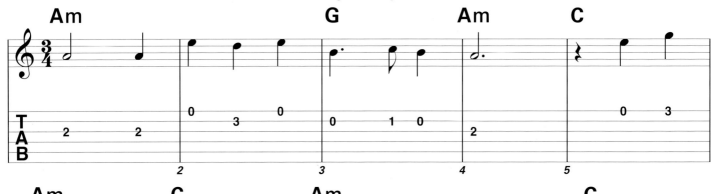

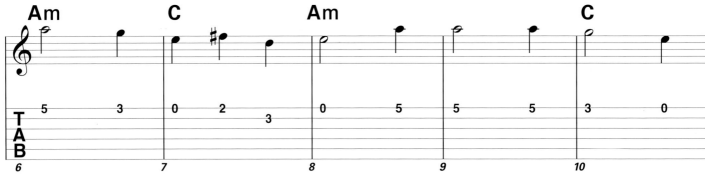

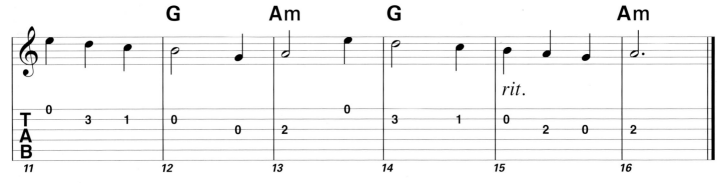

46 Auld Lang Syne

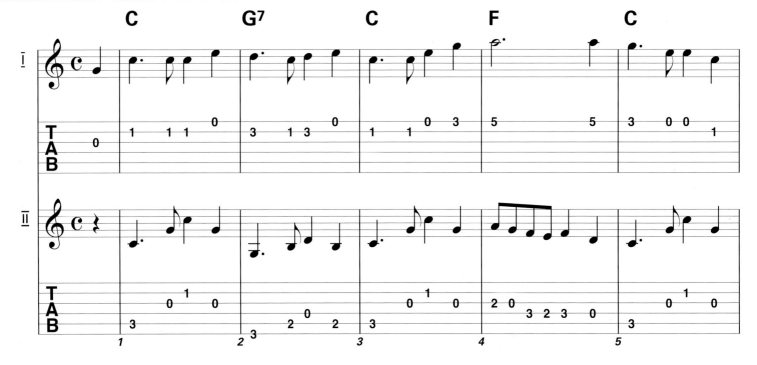

Suspended Chords

The chord symbol for a suspended chord is the major chord symbol plus the word **sus** (or sometimes **sus4**). The suspended chord is quite often used to add interest to a progression if there is a long section of music containing only one chord.

Dsus

D Suspended

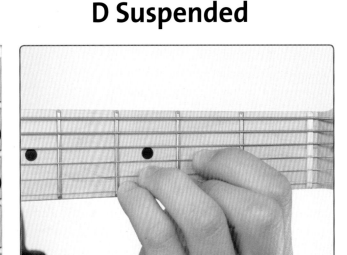

Dsus

Hold a **D major** chord shape then place your **fourth** finger on the **third** fret of the **1st** string.

The **open circle** on the chord diagram indicates that you hold the major chord shape and add the suspended note with your **fourth** finger. Suspended chords are nearly always played just before or just after the major chord, so it is easier to change between them if the major chord shape is held in position.

47.0

V ∧ V ∧ V ∧ V ∧
1 + 2 + 3 + 4 +

D   Dsus   D   Dsus

Asus

A Suspended

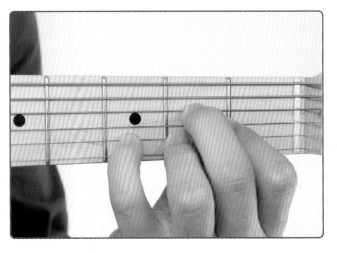

Asus

Hold an **A major** chord shape then place your **fourth** finger on the **third** fret of the **2nd** string.

Esus

E Suspended

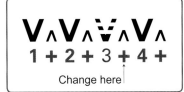

Esus

Hold an **E major** chord shape then place your **fourth** finger on the **second** fret of the **3rd** string.

This progression is two bars long. Change to the **E sus** chord (i.e. add your fourth finger) on the '**+**' after the 3 count.

The next progression contains all three of the **sus** chords you have learnt so far. Change to the **sus** chord on the '**+**' after the 2 count. Use **pivot** and **slide** fingers wherever possible between chord changes.

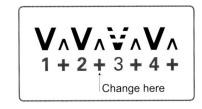

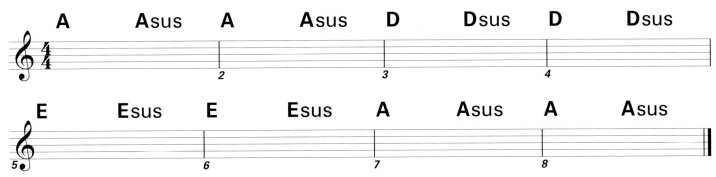

Here is a melody accompanied by the **sus** chords you have just learnt.

 48 **Suspended Blues**

www.learntoplaymusic.com

LESSON TWENTY-TWO

More on Bass Note Rhythm Patterns

In Lesson Nine you were introduced to bass note rhythm patterns in $\frac{3}{4}$ time. When playing a progression in $\frac{4}{4}$ time the following bass note rhythm patterns are commonly used.

Pick the bass note of the chord on the first beat and strum the first three or four strings of the chord on the 2nd, 3rd and 4th beats. Play the following bass note rhythm pattern holding a **G** chord shape.

 49.0

The best bass note to pick is the lowest note of the chord that has the same letter name of the chord. This is called the root note.

When playing a **G** type, pick the **6th** string note (**G note**), eg. G and G7 chords
When playing a **D** type, pick the **4th** string note (**D note**), eg. D, D7 and Dm chords
When playing a **C** type, pick the **5th** string note (**C note**), eg. C and C7 chords
When playing an **A** type, pick the **5th** string note (**A note**), eg. A, A7 and Am
When playing an **E** type, pick the **6th** string note (**E note**), eg. E, E7 and Em chords
When playing a **F** type, pick the **4th** string note (**F note**), eg. F chord

Practice this rhythm technique on each chord separately at first.
Remember to hold the full chord shape even though you are not playing all the strings.

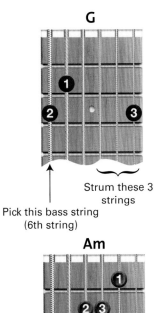

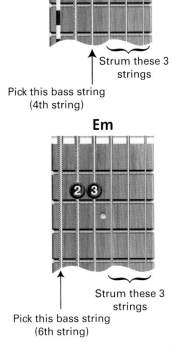

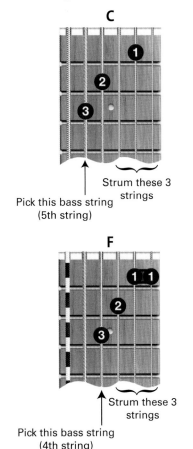

Play the following turnaround progression using bass note rhythm pattern 1.
Play the root note of the first beat of each bar.

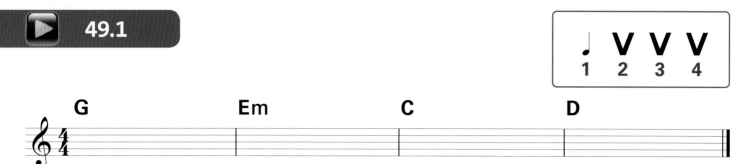

Now try a chord progression using a variation of bass note rhythm pattern 1 which contains **eighth** note strums on the second beat.

Bass Note Rhythm Pattern
Variation 1

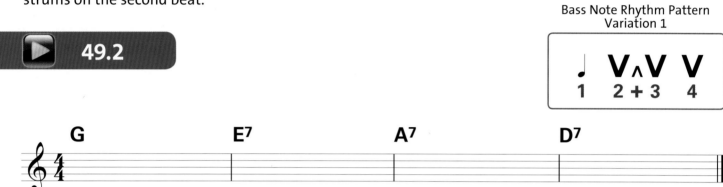

Bass Note Rhythm Pattern
Variation 2

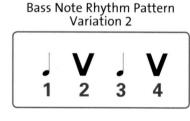

Another variation is to play the bass note on the first and third beats and strum on the second and fourth beats. Play the following bass note strum rhythm pattern, also holding a **G** chord shape. Play the root note of the chord on the first and third beats of the bar.

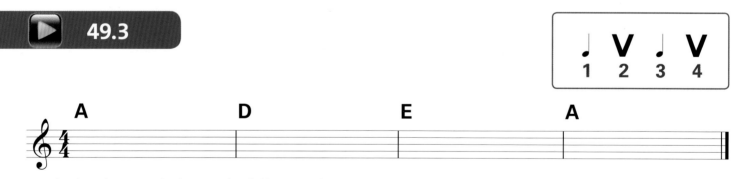

Apply the above variation to the following chord progression which contains two chords in each bar.

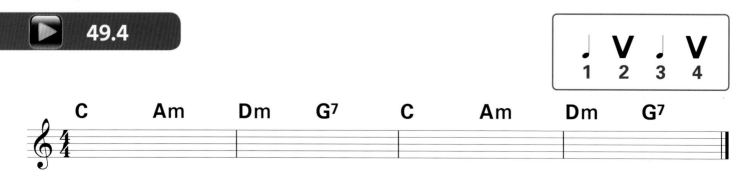

Once you are comfortable playing bass note rhythm patterns,
try using this technique to accompany the following melody.

 50   Arkansas Traveller

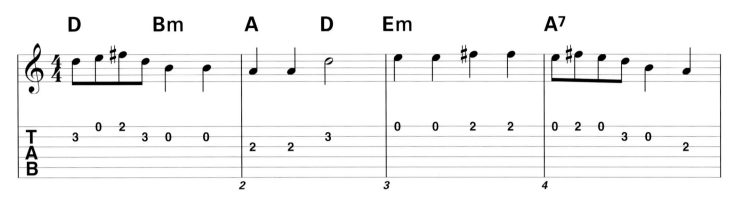

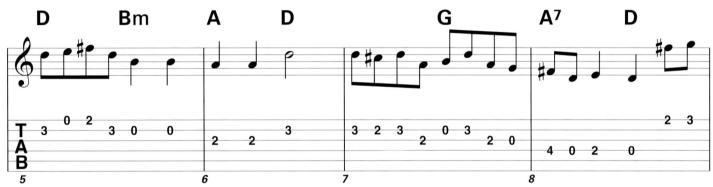

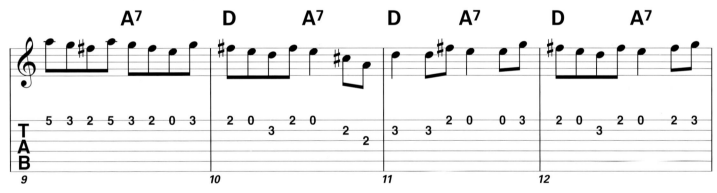

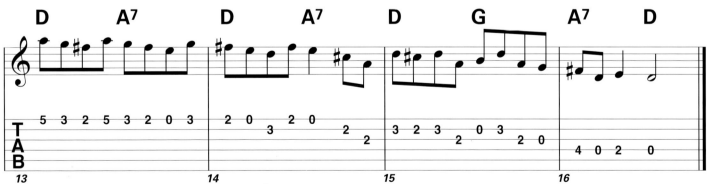

Alternate Bass Note Picking

In the previous examples the same bass note (the root note) is picked on the first and third beats. Another way of playing bass note picking is to alternate the bass notes. This rhythm is commonly used in Country music. You can alternate between any bass notes that are in the chord shapes. As long as you hold the chord shape while picking the bass notes it will sound correct.
Certain bass notes will sound better with certain chords. The best notes to use are the ones that sound good to your ear. It is usual to pick the root note on the first beat followed by a different bass note on the third beat. Use alternate bass note picking in the following chord progression. You can also experiment playing different bass notes than the ones suggested.

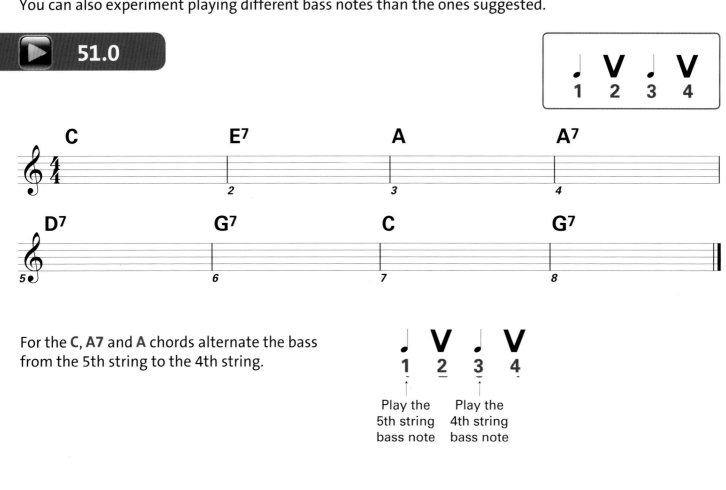

For the **C**, **A7** and **A** chords alternate the bass from the 5th string to the 4th string.

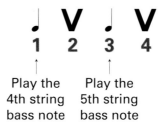

For the **D7** chord alternate between the 4th string bass note and the 5th string bass note.

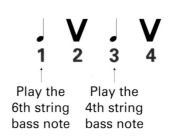

For the **G7** and **E7** chords alternate between the 6th string bass note and the 4th string bass note.

Practice each chord shape separately at first and experiment using alternate bass note picking on other progressions.

51.1   God Rest Ye Merry Gentlemen

When playing the accompaniment to this song, you could use an alternate bass note on the third beat of each bar.

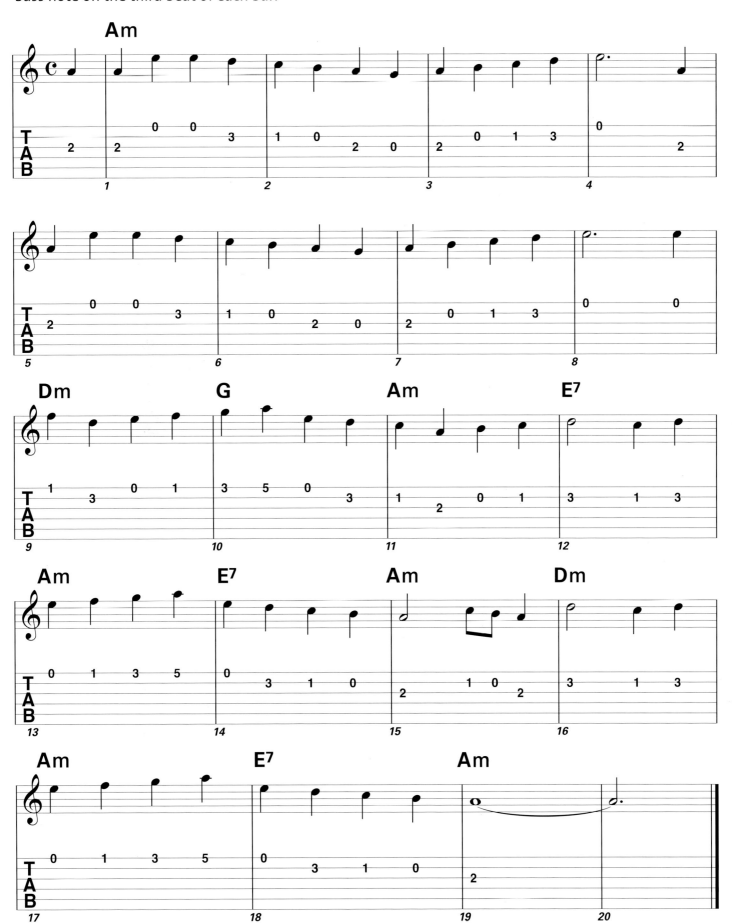

LESSON TWENTY-THREE

The Major Scale

The **major scale** is a series of **8** notes in alphabetical order that has the familiar sound:

Do	Re	Mi	Fa	So	La	Ti	Do

The **C major scale** contains the following notes.

Note Name	C	D	E	F	G	A	B	C
Interval	tone T	tone T	semitone ST	tone T	tone T	tone T	semitone ST	

The distance between each note is two frets except for **EF** and **BC** where the distance is only one fret.

The distance of two frets is called a **tone** (sometimes called a **step**), indicated by **T**.

The distance of one fret is called a **semitone** (sometimes called a **half step**), indicated by **S**.

The first note and last note of a major scale always have the same name.
In the **C major** scale the distance from the lowest C to the C note above it is **one octave** (8 notes).
The following example is one octave of the C major scale.

> ▶ **52.0   The C Major Scale**

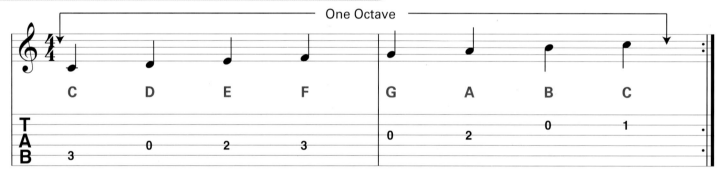

Each of the 8 notes in the major scale is given a **scale number** (or **degree**)

Note Name	C	D	E	F	G	A	B	C
Interval	tone T	tone T	semitone ST	tone T	tone T	tone T	semitone ST	

The distance between two notes is called an **interval**.

In any major scale the interval between the 3rd to 4th note and the 7th to 8th note in the scale is one semitone (1 fret) apart. All other notes are one tone (2 frets) apart.

The Key Of C Major

When a song consists of notes from a particular scale, it is said to be written in the **key** which has the same notes as that scale. For example, if a song contains mostly notes from the **C major scale**, it is said to be in the **key of C major**. The songs you have played in this book that commence with a **C** chord written above the first bar of music are in the **key of C major**.

Morning Has Broken is a well known folk song. It is written here in the key of **C major**.

In any particular key, certain chords are more common than others, and after a while you will become familiar with the chords that belong to each key. Certain keys are easier for guitarists to play in and you should learn how to transpose (change the key of a song) so you can change a song that is in a difficult key (contains lots of sharps and flats or difficult chord shapes for a beginner to play) into an easier key. The most common chords in the key of C major are;

C   Dm   Em   F   G7   Am

For more information on transposing and chords, see Progressive Guitar Method: Rhythm.

LESSON TWENTY-FOUR

The G Major Scale

The **G major** scale starts and ends on the note **G** and contains an **F sharp** (F♯) note. Written below are two octaves of the **G major** scale. Notice that the **G major** scale has the same patterns of tones and semitones as the **C major** scale. In a major scale the interval between the 3rd to 4th note and the 7th to 8th notes is a semitone (1 fret). In the **G major** scale, to keep this pattern of tones and semitones correct, an F♯ note must be used instead of an F note.

> ▶ **53.0   The G Major Scale over Two Octaves**

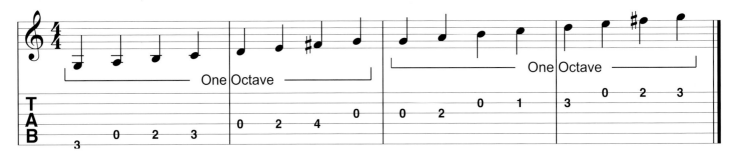

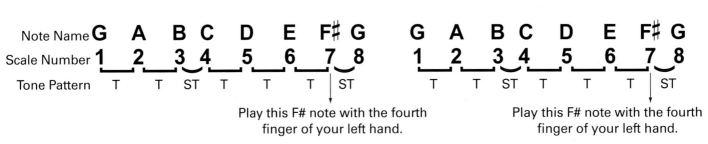

Note Name	G	A	B	C	D	E	F♯	G	G	A	B	C	D	E	F♯	G
Scale Number	1	2	3	4	5	6	7	8	1	2	3	4	5	6	7	8
Tone Pattern	T	T	ST	T	T	T	ST		T	T	ST	T	T	T	ST	

Play this F# note with the fourth finger of your left hand.

Play this F# note with the fourth finger of your left hand.

Songs in the key of C major use notes from the C major scale, songs in the key of G major use notes from the G major scale, so songs in the key of G major will contain F sharp (F♯) notes rather than F.

Key Signatures

Instead of writing a sharp sign before every F note on the staff, it is easier to write just one sharp sign after each clef. This means that all the F notes on the staff are played as F♯, even though there is no sharp sign written before them.
This is called a **key signature**.

C Major Key signature

The **C major** scale contains no sharps or flats, therefore the key signature for the key of **C major** contains no sharps or flats.

G Major Key signature

The **G major** scale contains one sharp, F♯, therefore the key signature for the key of **G major** contains one sharp, F♯.

www.learntoplaymusic.com

The most common chords in the key of G major are;

G   Am   Bm   C   D7   Em

The following songs 'All Through the Night' and 'Lavender's Blue' are in the key of G major.
The key signature tells you that all F notes on the music are played as F sharp (F♯).

These songs contain all the common chords in the key of G major.

53.1   All Through the Night

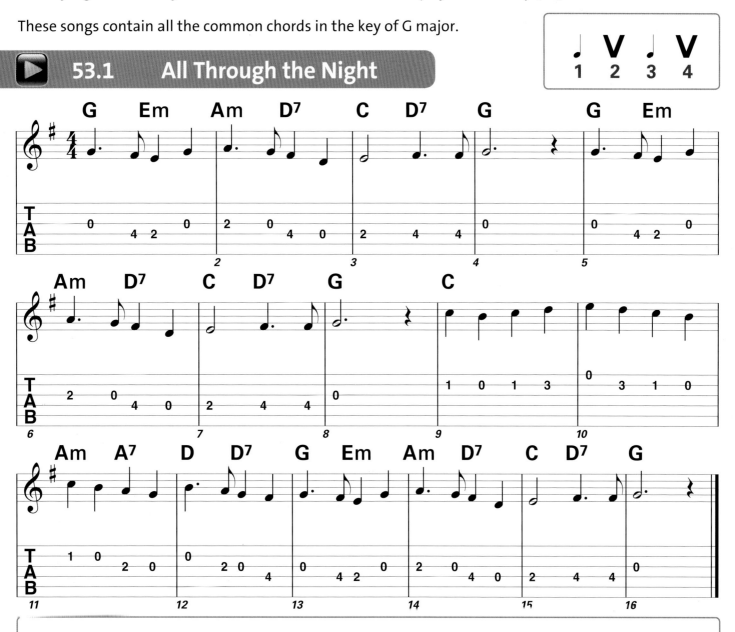

Know your Guitars...
Gibson 335

Many Blues and Jazz players favor hollow body electric guitars for their full, rich tone. One of the most famous hollow body electrics is the Gibson 335. It has been used by players like Freddy King, Magic Sam and Larry Carlton. BB King had a model called the 345 specially designed for him. His guitar is named Lucille.

Know your Guitars…

Gibson Les Paul

Along with the Fender Stratocaster, the Gibson Les Paul is one of the most famous of all electric guitars. It is great for heavy Rock sounds as well as as being versatile enough for Blues and Jazz. This guitar was made specially for Les Paul - a great Jazz player who also invented multitrack recording. This technique is essential for recording and is now used by everyone from top recording studios to musicians using computers at home.

LESSON TWENTY-FIVE

The F Major Scale

All major scales have the same pattern of tones and semitones, i.e. the interval between the 3rd and 4th note and the 7th to 8th note in the scale is a semitone (1 fret). For the **F major** scale to keep this pattern of tones and semitones a **B flat (B♭)** note must be used instead of a **B** note.

 54.0   The F Major Scale over Two Octaves

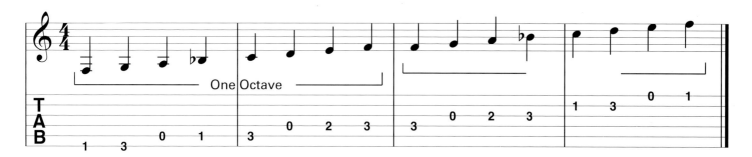

Note Name	**F**	**G**	**A**	**B♭**	**C**	**D**	**E**	**F**	**F**	**G**	**A**	**B♭**	**C**	**D**	**E**	**F**
Scale Number	**1**	**2**	**3**	**4**	**5**	**6**	**7**	**8**	**1**	**2**	**3**	**4**	**5**	**6**	**7**	**8**
Tone Pattern		T	T	ST	T	T	T	ST		T	T	ST	T	T	T	ST

Songs in the key of F major use notes from the F major scale, so songs in the key of F major will contain B flat (B♭) notes rather than B.

F Major Key signature

The **F major** scale contains one flat B♭, therefore the key signature for the key of **F major** contains one flat, B♭.

The most common chords in the key of F major are;

F   Gm   Am   B♭   C7   Dm

54.1   The Galway Piper

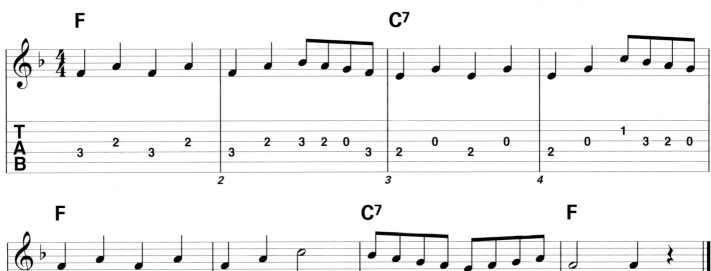

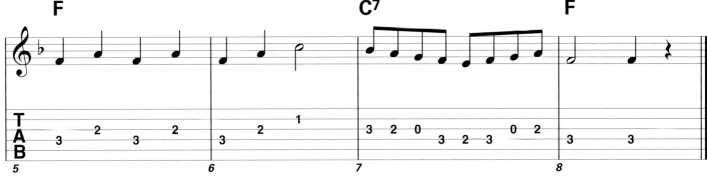

54.2   Mary Ann

www.learntoplaymusic.com

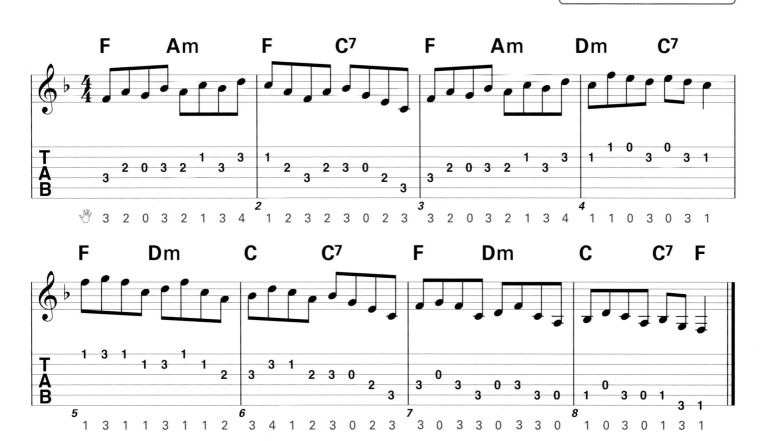

Know your Guitars…
Acoustic Cutaway

As well as the standard acoustic guitar, there is another version called a Cutaway where part of the body of the guitar is cut back and reshaped along the side of the fretboard. This makes it easier to play notes high up on the fretboard, which is great for playing Lead solos on an acoustic guitar. Many players who switch frequently between acoustic and electric prefer to use an acoustic cutaway.

LESSON TWENTY-SIX

The Eighth Rest

 This symbol is an **eighth rest.** It indicates **half a beat** of silence.

▶ 55.0

There are two common positions for eighth note rests: off the beat and on the beat. These are demonstrated in the following example.

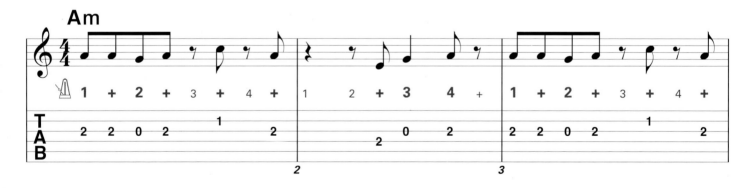

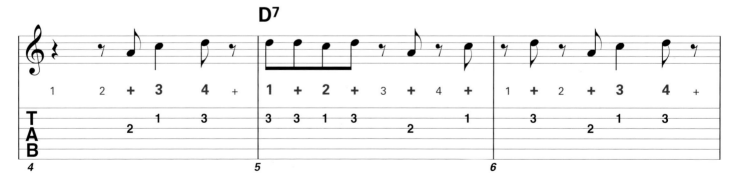

Syncopation

Syncopation occurs when notes are played "off" the beat, i.e. when notes are not played on the number part of the count but on the '+' part of the count.

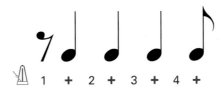

A tie can also be used to create a syncopated feel, by moving the accent (emphasis) off the beat.

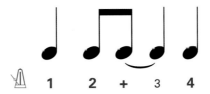

The syncopation in the following songs is created by using both of the above methods.

Electric Guitar Pickups…

Humbuckers

Although single coil pickups make a great sound, they can also produce unwanted noise known as hum. In the 1950's, guitar makers discovered that if you put two single coil pickups together, the second one cancels the hum, as well as producing a fatter, warmer sound. Thus the humbucking pickup (Humbucker) was born. These pickups are traditionally associated with Gibson guitars such as the Les Paul and the 335.

56 **Jamaica Farewell**

LESSON TWENTY-SEVEN

Alternative Chord Shapes

There are many different chord shapes that can be used for a particular chord type. Here are some common alternative chord shapes that you should learn. Apply these new shapes to the progressions in this lesson and earlier lessons. Certain chord shapes sound better or are easier to play in some chord progressions than others.

E7

E Seventh

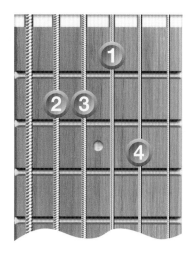
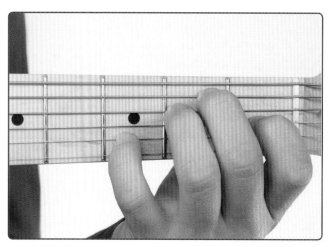

E7

This **E7** shape is an **E** chord with an additional note played by the fourth finger.

A7

A Seventh

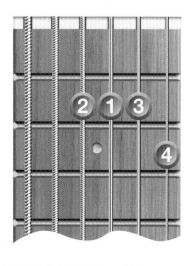
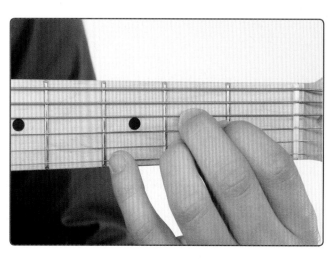

A7

This **A7** shape is an **A** chord with an additional note played by the fourth finger.

▶ 57.0

V	V	V	V
1	2	3	4

Major Sixth Chords

Major sixth chords are more commonly referred to as sixth chords.
The chord symbol for the sixth chord is the major chord symbol followed by the number 6.

E6

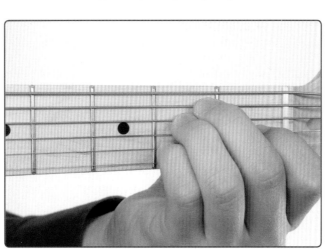

E Sixth Chord

The E6 chord shape is an E chord with the additional note played by the fourth finger.

In the following chord progression use the alternative E7 chord shape given in the previous lesson.
Hold the E chord shape throughout and move only the fourth finger to change chords.

A6

A Sixth Chord

A6

The A6 chord shape is an A chord with the additional note played by the fourth finger. Another way of playing this shape is to bar all four strings with the first finger.

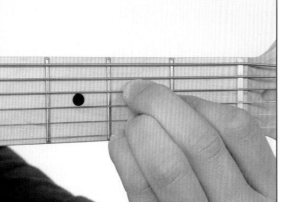

In the progression below use the above fingering for the A6 chord. For the A7 chord,
just slide the fourth finger to the third fret of the 1st string. This will make the chord change easier.

| A | A6 | A7 | A6 | A | A6 | A7 | A6 |

Play this Blues in **E** using the previous two progressions. There are four chords in each bar,
each receiving one strum, except bars **9** and **12** where a **B7** chord is played.

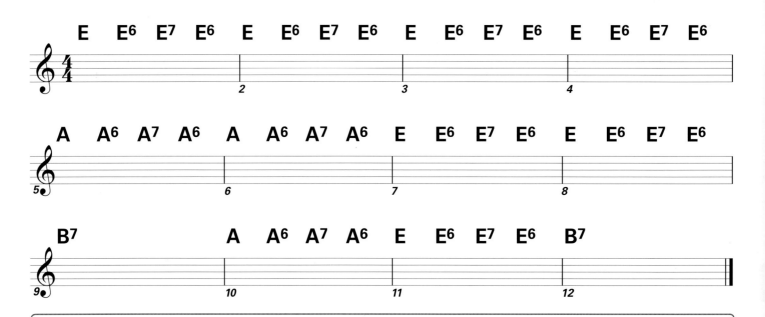

Know Your Guitars...
Larrivee Parlor Guitar

The Larrivee Parlor guitar has a smaller body and shorter neck than standard acoustic guitars. This means the frets are closer together, making it easier for people with smaller hands to play. Despite its size, this guitar is surprisingly loud and has a beautiful tone. It's particularly good for Folk, Ragtime and Country Blues. Because of its smaller size, the Larrivee Parlor guitar was chosen as the staff guitar on the International Space Station.

LESSON TWENTY-EIGHT

Rock Chords

When playing Rock or Blues styles, guitarists commonly use chords where only two strings are played. These two note chords are called **Rock chords** (also known as 'Fifth chords' or 'Power chords' and are useful as alternative shapes for major, sixth, and seventh chords).

A Rock Chord Shapes

Here are the two string Rock chord shapes for **A**, **A6** and **A7**. In all three chord shapes only the 5th and 4th strings are strummed.

A

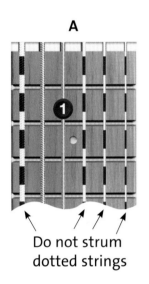

Do not strum dotted strings

A6

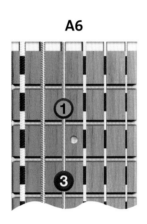

A7

The open circle with the number 1 inside it indicates that you keep your 1st finger in position even though that note is not being played.

Play the following chord progression using the above rock chord shapes.
Use eighth note strums and only play the 5th and 4th strings. Use only down strums as this sounds better when playing the Rock chords in the following examples.

 58.0

 58.1

Play examples 58.0 and 58.1 as a two bar pattern.

A A A⁶ A A A A⁶ A A A A⁶ A A⁷ A A⁶ A

D Rock Chord Shapes

Here are the two string rock chord shapes for **D**, **D6** and **D7**.
Play only the **4th** and **3rd** strings.

D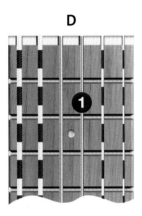

D6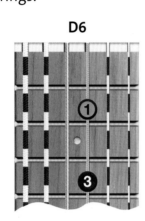

D7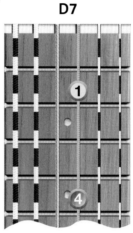

Play the following two bar chord progression using the **D** rock chord shapes.
Use only downward eighth note strums, playing the 4th and 3rd strings only.

 58.3

D D D⁶ D D D D⁶ D D D D⁶ D D⁷ D D⁶ D

E Rock Chord Shapes

Here are the two string rock chord shapes for **E**, **E6** and **E7**.
Play only the **6th** and **5th** strings.

E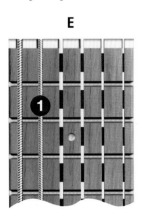

E6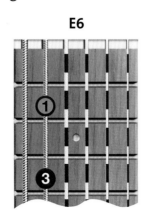

E7

Play the following two bar chord progression using the rock chord shapes on the previous page. Use only downward eighth note strums.

58.4

| E | E | E⁶ | E | E | E | E⁶ | E | E | E | E⁶ | E | E⁷ | E | E⁶ | E |

58.5   **12 Bar Blues in A**

Play the following 12 bar Blues in the key of **A** using rock chords. When there are two bars of a chord, substitute the two bar rock progressions above. Eg: for the **A** chord in bars 1 and 2, 3 and 4, 7 and 8, use the two bar progression in example 58.2. For the **D** chord in bars 5 and 6, use the two bar progression in example 58.3. For each chord in the last four bars, substitute the second half of the rock chord progression. Try to play this 12 bar Blues from memory. If you hope to play in a band or even jam with friends, the ability to play songs from memory is an important skill to develop.

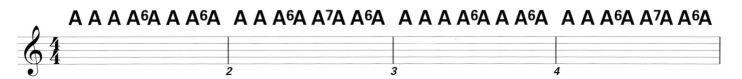

Guitar Effects...
Loop Pedal

A great tool for both acoustic and electric guitar is the Loop pedal, which is basically a mini recording machine controlled by your foot. Plugging your guitar into a loop pedal enables you to play a chord progression and then get the pedal to loop it (repeat it) while you play another part or improvise over what you have just recorded.

The rock chord pattern from the previous example can be used as an accompaniment to this Rock and Roll style Blues solo. Play the solo while your teacher or a friend plays the rhythm part and then swap over. This is essentially what 'jamming' is all about.

LESSON TWENTY-NINE

Eighth Note Triplet Rhythms

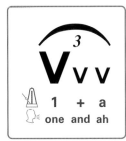

Eighth note triplet rhythms are **three** evenly spaced strums within one beat.
One bar of eighth note triplets in $\frac{4}{4}$ time would consist of **four** groups of **three** strums.
There are **12 strums** per bar but still only **four beats.** Accent (play louder) the first downstrum of each group of three strums.

 60.0

Play the following rhythm pattern holding a **C** chord.

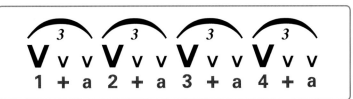

 60.1

Now use the triplet rhythm pattern on a chord progression.

D	Bm	Em	A⁷

 60.2

This example uses a triplet rhythm on the **second** beat only.

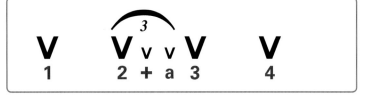

D	Bm	Em	A⁷

60.3

This one uses a triplet rhythm on the **second** and **third** beats.

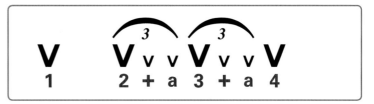

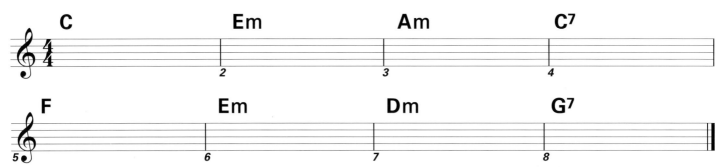

Arpeggio playing

All the previous rhythm patterns you have played used strums. Another method of playing chords is by picking each string individually. This is called **arpeggio** playing.

Hold a **C** chord shape. Pick each string in the following order and use triplet timing. Remember to pick each string one at a time.

When playing arpeggio style it helps to support your right hand by placing your ring and little fingers on the body of the guitar as shown in the photos below. This will keep your hand steady and help you achieve a smooth, even sound.

Finger support on electric.

Finger support on acoustic.

61.0

Try arpeggio picking the following chord progression.

The first note picked is usually the root note of the chord. Strings can be picked in any order you wish. As long as you are holding a chord shape it will sound correct. Some picking patterns sound better than others in different progressions. This arpeggio style of playing can be used on any chord progression.

Apply the same arpeggio picking pattern to the following chord progression containing 4 bars of music and 2 chords in each bar. Pick the root note of the chord first and use the alternative **E7** chord shape introduced on page 108.

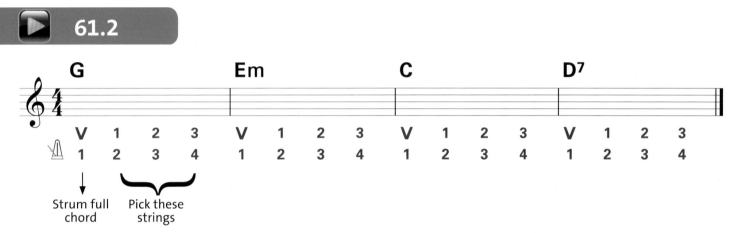

The following example does not use triplet timing. Strum the full chord on the first beat followed by the 1st, 2nd and 3rd strings on the second, third and fourth beats while holding the chord shape.

61.2

Combining Strumming and Arpeggio Patterns

Try the following rhythm pattern which picks the root note of the chord followed by strums for the first bar and arpeggio picking for the second bar. Use a **G** chord in $\frac{3}{4}$ time.

61.3

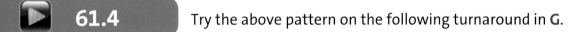

61.4 Try the above pattern on the following turnaround in **G**.

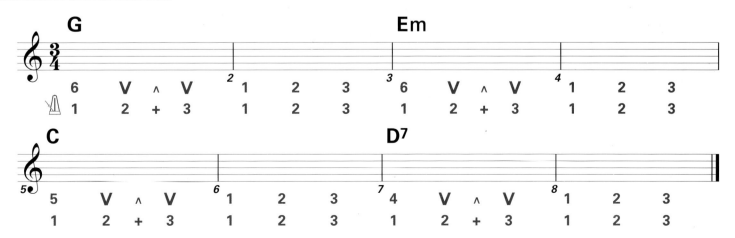

LESSON THIRTY

More About Arpeggios

An arpeggio is a chord played one note at a time. The value of arpeggios is that they enable you to play parts which fit chord progressions perfectly, since every note of an arpeggio is a note of the accompanying chord. Written below is a C major arpeggio which consists of the notes C, E and G. These are the root, third and fifth of a C major chord. To play this arpeggio, simply hold down a C chord shape and pick the notes individually.

▶ **62.0**

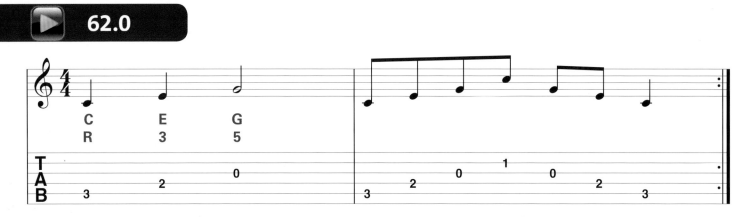

Here is another example which makes use of arpeggios. Hold down the chord shapes indicated as much as possible, except when playing notes which are not in the chords (e.g. the B note at the end of bar 2). Take care with your picking and make sure all your notes are clear and even.

▶ **62.1**

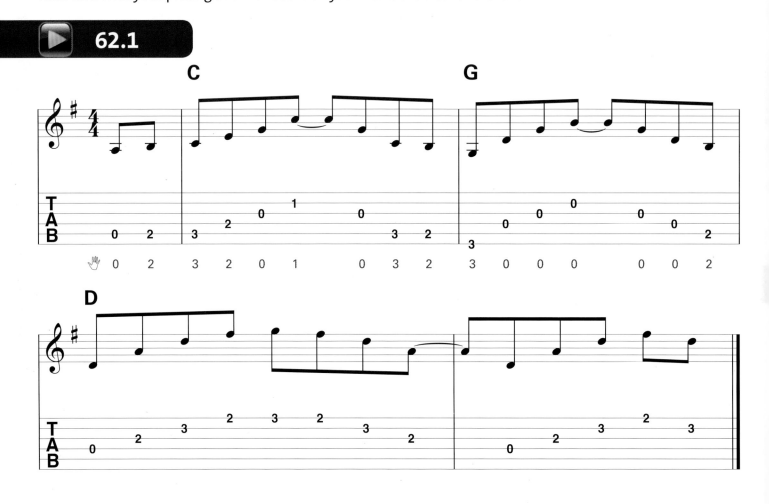

Minor Arpeggios

For every type of chord there is a corresponding arpeggio. Shown below is an A minor arpeggio.

62.2   A Minor Arpeggio

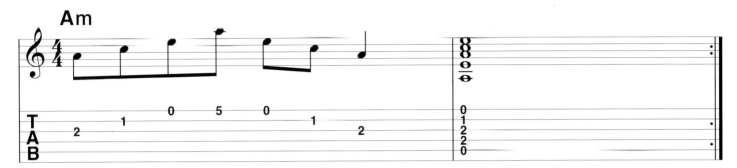

62.3

This example contains both major and minor arpeggios.

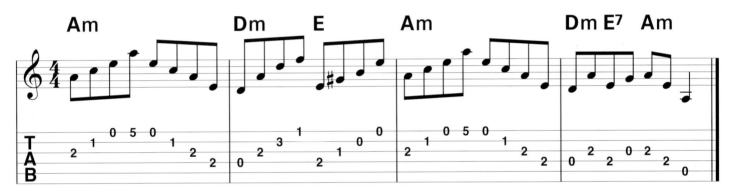

Augmented and Diminished Chords

Two more interesting types of chords are augmented (+) and diminished (o) chords. These are not as common as major or minor chords, but they are often used as a way of creating tension before resolving to either a major or minor chord. Here are some examples demonstrating these chords. Listen to the recording to hear what they sound like.

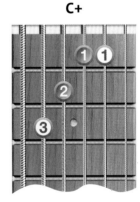

C+

62.4   C Augmented

62.5   C Diminished

Cdim

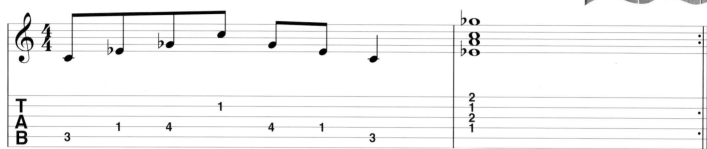

62.6

This example contains arpeggios of four types of chords — **major**, **minor**, **augmented** and **diminished**.

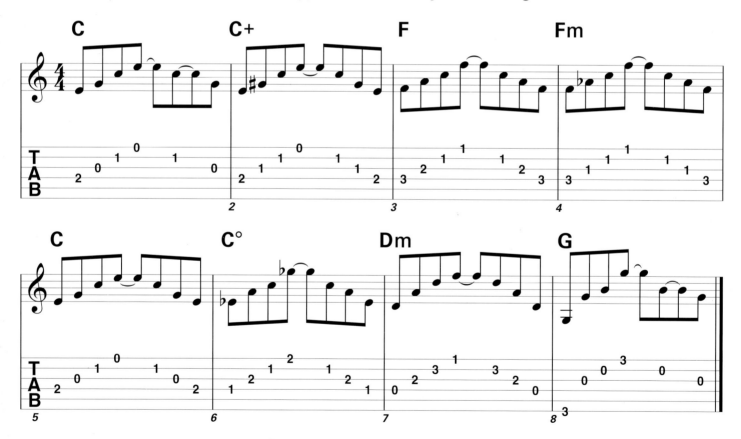

LESSON THIRTY-ONE

Minor Keys and Scales

Apart from major keys, the other basic tonality used in western music is a **minor key**. Minor keys are often said to have a sadder or darker sound than major keys. Songs in a minor key use notes taken from a **minor scale**. There are three types of minor scale — the **natural minor scale**, the **harmonic minor scale** and the **melodic minor scale**. Written below is the **A natural minor** scale.

The Natural Minor Scale

The **A natural minor** scale contains exactly the same notes as the **C major** scale. The difference is that it starts and finishes on an **A** note instead of a C note. The A note then becomes the key note. To highlight the difference, the degrees of the scale as they would relate to the A major scale are written under the note names. Notice the **flattened 3rd, 6th and 7th**.

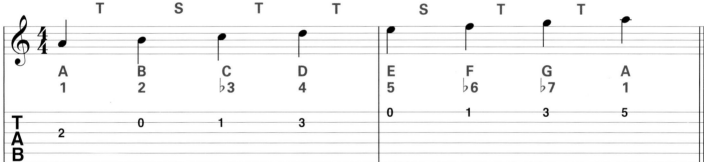

Here is the full fingering for the **A natural minor** scale in the open position, moving up to the high A at the 5th fret on the first string. Learn it from memory and then play it with your eyes closed, naming the notes out loud, and then naming the scale degrees out loud.

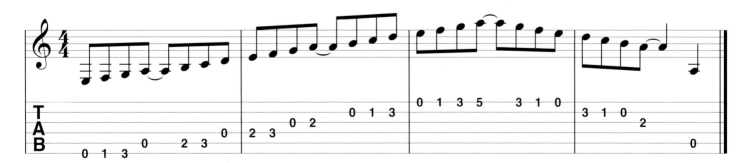

Here is a melody in the **key of A minor** which is derived from the **A natural minor scale**.
Above bar 16, the instruction D.C. al Fine is written. This means you play again from the beginning until you reach the word *Fine* (bar 8).

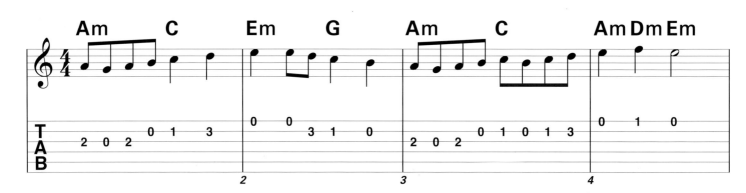

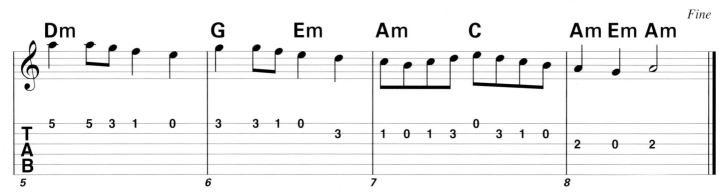

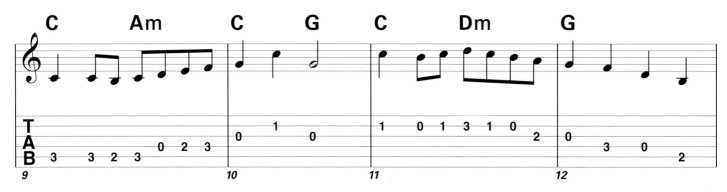

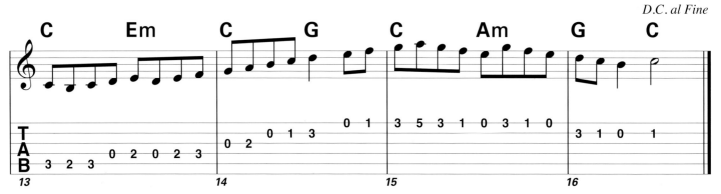

The Harmonic Minor Scale

The **harmonic minor** scale has a distance of 1½ tones between the **6th** and **7th** degrees.
The raised 7th degree is the only difference between the harmonic minor and the natural minor.
This scale is often described as having an "Eastern" sound.

 65.0   A Harmonic Minor

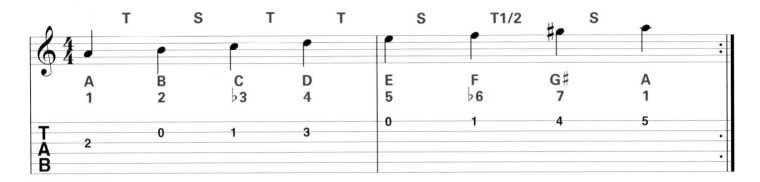

 65.1

This example is derived from the notes of the **A harmonic minor** scale.

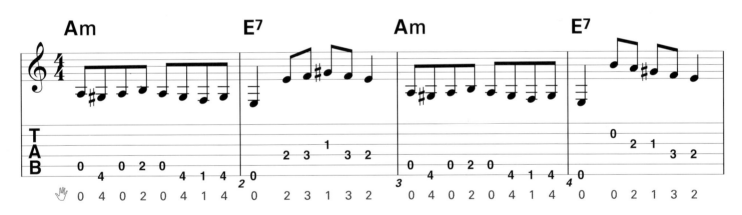

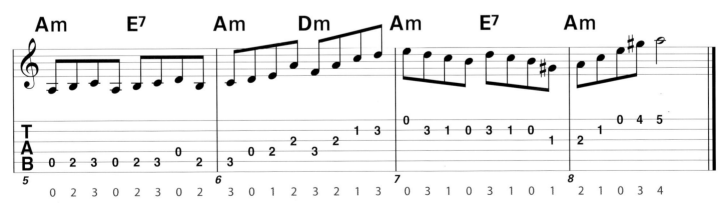

The Melodic Minor Scale

In the **A melodic minor** scale the **6th** and **7th** notes are sharpened when ascending and returned to natural when descending. This is the way the melodic minor is used in Classical music. However, in Jazz and other more modern styles, the melodic minor often descends the same way it ascends. An easy way to think of the ascending melodic minor is as a major scale with a flattened third degree.

 66.0   A Melodic Minor

 66.1

When playing music in minor keys, it is common to use notes and chords from all three types of minor scales. Here is an example. This example also contains one chromatic note (A♯ or B♭) as part of a repeating bass run.

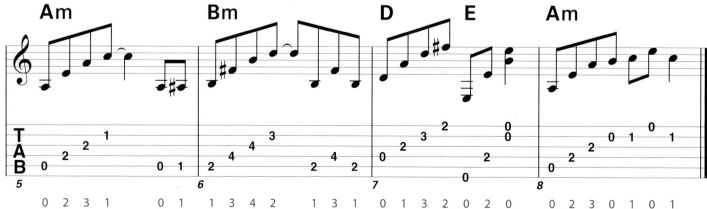

Relative Keys

If you compare the **A natural minor** scale with the **C major** scale you will notice that they contain the same notes. The only difference is that they start on a different note. Because of this, these two scales are referred to as "relatives"; **A minor** is the **relative minor** of **C major** and vice versa.

Major Scale: C Major

Relative Minor Scale: A Natural Minor

The harmonic and melodic minor scale variations are also relatives of the same major scale, for example, the **A harmonic** and **A melodic minor** scales are both relatives of **C major**. For every major scale (and every major chord) there is a relative minor scale which is based upon the **6th note** of the major scale. This is outlined in the table below.

Major Key (I)	C	D♭	D	E♭	E	F	F♯	G♭	G	A♭	A	B♭	B
Relative Minor Key (VI)	Am	B♭m	Bm	Cm	C♯m	Dm	D♯m	E♭m	Em	Fm	F♯m	Gm	G♯m

Both the major and the relative minor share the same key signature, as illustrated below.

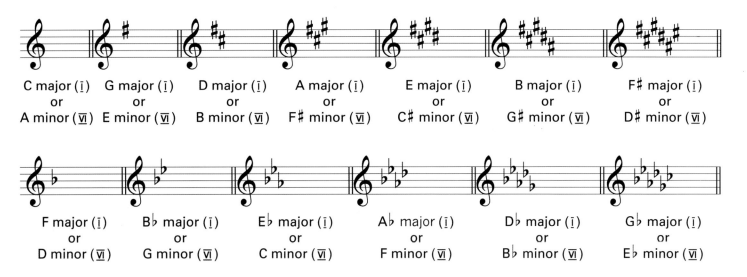

To determine whether a song is in a major key or the relative minor key, look at the last note or chord of the song. Songs often finish on the root note or the root chord which indicates the key.

For example, if the key signature contained one sharp, and the last chord of the song was **Em**, the key would probably be **E minor**, not **G major**. Minor key signatures are always based on the natural minor scale. The sharpened 6th and 7th degrees from the harmonic and melodic minor scales are not indicated in the key signature. This usually means there are accidentals (temporary sharps, flats or naturals) in melodies created from these scales.

Slash Chords

In the following example, you will notice some new chord symbols. These symbols indicate a chord with a specific bass note under it, and are called slash chords. E.g. in bar 2, the chord symbol **G/B** occurs. This indicates a **G** chord played over a **B** bass note. In bar 4, the symbol **C/E** indicates a **C** chord over an **E** bass note. Slash chords are often used to create smooth, melodic bass lines and the symbols tell you that a note other than the root is played as the bass note of the chord.

Slash chords can create many different harmonic effects. Each combination has a specific name and often creates an entirely new chord. Basically you can play any chord over any bass note as long as it sounds good. Experiment with playing all the chords you have learnt over various bass notes from the scale of the key you are playing in.

> ▶ **67** **Spiral Staircase**

This example alternates between the relative keys of **C major** and **A minor**. The arpeggio style of playing used here is particularly effective when playing a ballad. This piece contains some new chord symbols. These indicate a chord with a specific bass note under it, and are called **slash chords**. For example, in the first full bar, the chord symbol **G/B** occurs. This indicates a **G** chord played **over** a **B** bass note.

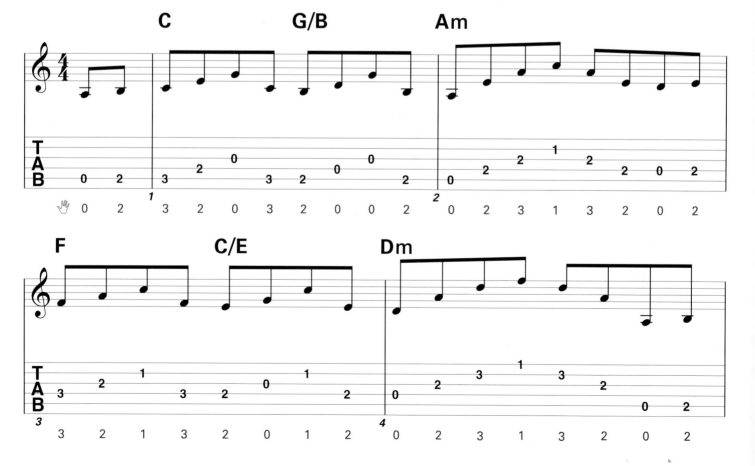

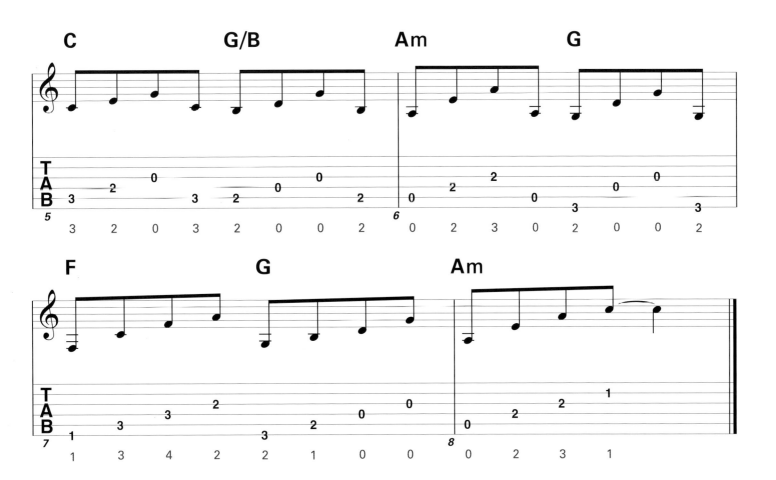

Classic Amps…
The Marshall Stack

The most famous Rock guitar amp of them all, the Marshall 100 watt amp with a 4x12 inch speaker "Quad box" has been widely used since it was invented by Jim Marshall in the 1960's. The term "stack" means an amp sitting on top of a separate speaker box. Marshall amps produce great overdriven sounds which are perfect for both Rhythm and Lead Rock guitar.

LESSON THIRTY-THREE

The Six Eight Time Signature

$\frac{6}{8}$

This is the **six eight** time signature.
There are six eighth notes in one bar of $\frac{6}{8}$ time.
The six eighth notes are divided into two groups of three.

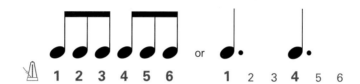

In $\frac{6}{8}$ time there are **two** pulses within each bar, with each beat being a **dotted quarter note.**
(This is different to $\frac{4}{4}$ and $\frac{3}{4}$ time where each beat is a quarter note).
Accent (play louder) the 1 and 4 count to help establish the two pulses per bar.

> **68.0   House of the Rising Sun**

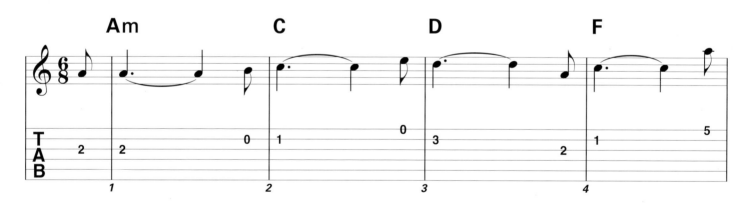

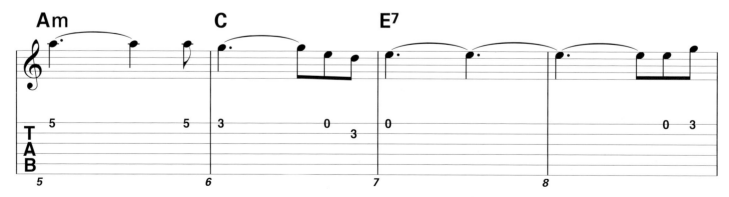

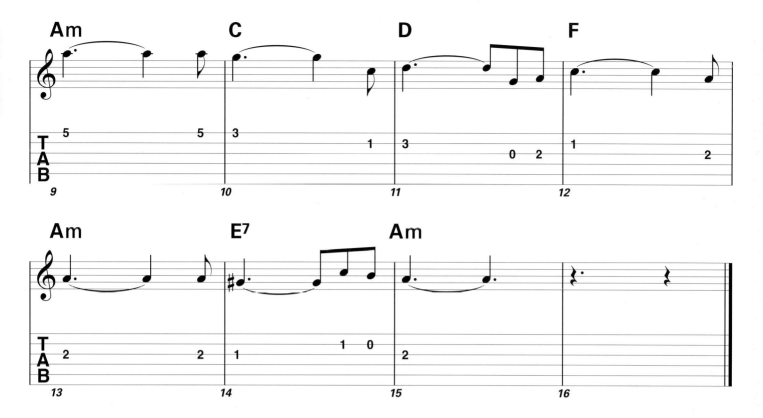

The songs 'House of the Rising Sun' and 'When Johnny Comes Marching Home' are in the **key of A minor (Am)**. The notes used in these songs are from the A minor scale. The key signature for the key of A minor is the same as C major, that is it contains no sharps or flats.

C Major Key Signature

A Minor Key Signature

It is common for songs in the key of A minor to contain a **G sharp** (G♯) in its melody as in bar 14 of House of the Rising Sun. For more information on minor scales see Progressive Guitar Method:Theory.

Know your Guitars…
Martin Dreadnought

In the early part of the 20th century, guitar manufacturer C.F. Martin released an acoustic guitar with a larger, deeper body than most existing guitars. Around the same time, the British navy launched a battleship that was so big it would fear nothing. It was called "HMS Dreadnought". Martin thought this would be a good name for his new guitar.
The guitar sounded great and the name caught on. Today, the dreadnought is the most commonly used type of acoustic guitar in the world.

Here is an arpeggio style accompaniment for 'House of the Rising Sun'. Look through the chords and see which ones come from each type of minor scale. Try playing this accompaniment while a friend plays the melody on another guitar. To be a good guitarist, you need to be able to play both the chords and melody of all the songs you learn. This is the basis of rhythm and lead guitar.

▶ 68.1 House of the Rising Sun

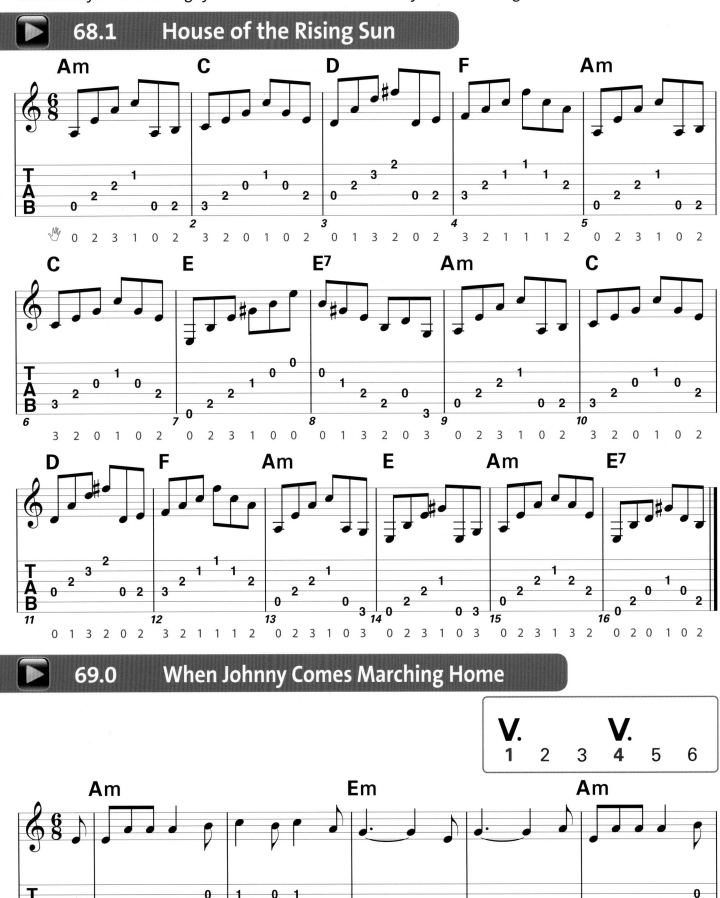

▶ 69.0 When Johnny Comes Marching Home

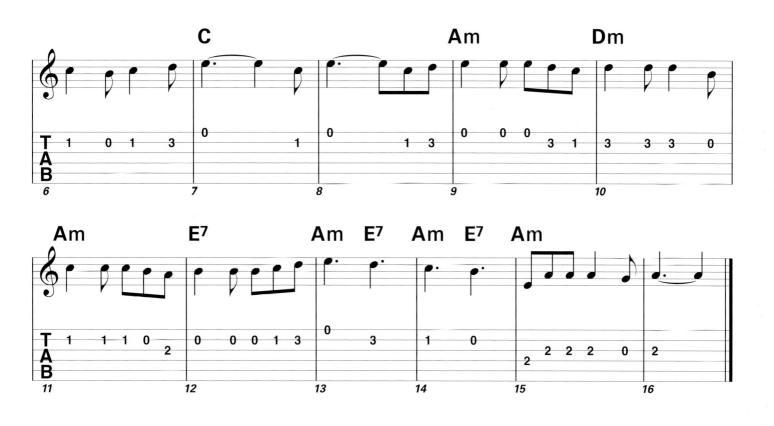

69.1   The Irish Washerwoman

V.
1 2 3 4 5 6

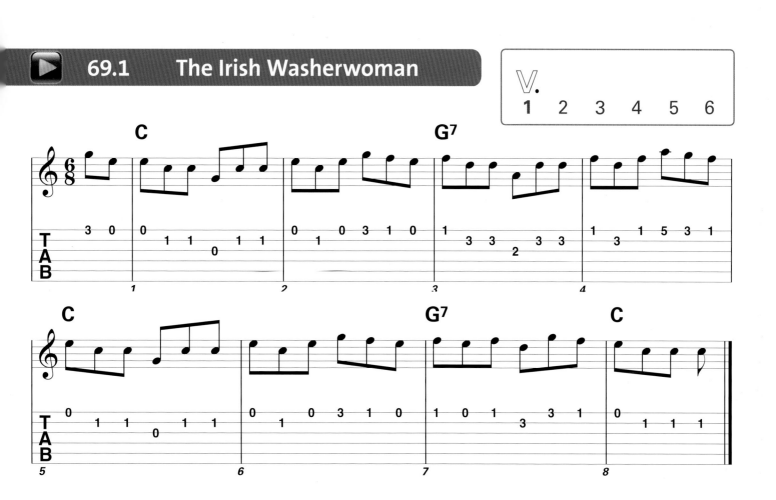

LESSON THIRTY-FOUR

The Eighth Note Triplet

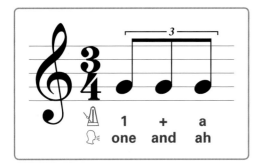

Eighth note **triplets** are a group of **three** evenly spaced notes played within one beat. Eighth note triplets are indicated by three eighth notes grouped together by a bracket (or a curved line) and the number *3* written either above or below the group.

The eighth note triplets are played with a third of a beat each.
To help you keep time, **Accent** (play louder) the first note of each triplet group.

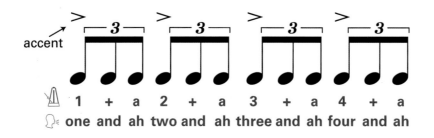

▶ 70.0

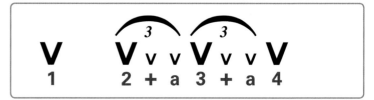

Shuffle Rhythm

The shuffle rhythm is created by playing the first and third notes of the triplet group. In music notation the shuffle rhythm is often indicated by an eighth rest replacing the middle note of the triplet.

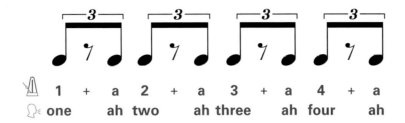

In the blues below the first beat of each bar is played as a shuffle rhythm with the remaining three beats of the bar played as eighth note triplets. To achieve the eighth rest, place your left hand fingers lightly on the strings.

As a suggestion, perhaps use the Rock chords learnt in Lesson 28 to accompany this song.

 70.1   Shuffle Your Feet

Swing Rhythms

A **swing rhythm** can be created by tying the first two notes of the triplet group together.

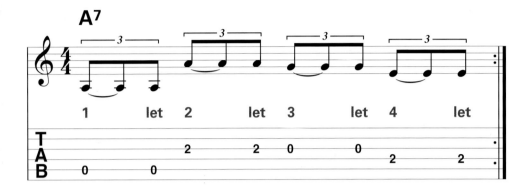

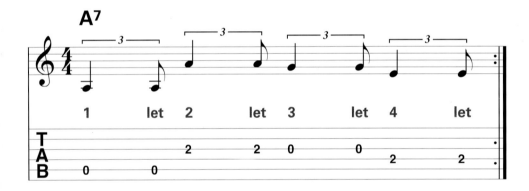

The two eighth note triplets tied together in the example above can be replaced by a quarter note.

To simplify notation, it is common to replace the with ♩♪,

and to write at the start of the piece as illustrated below.

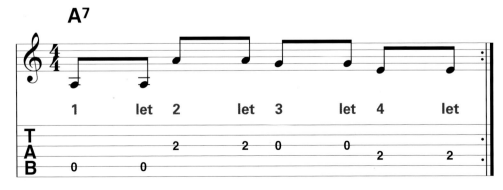

72.0   **Rock My Soul**

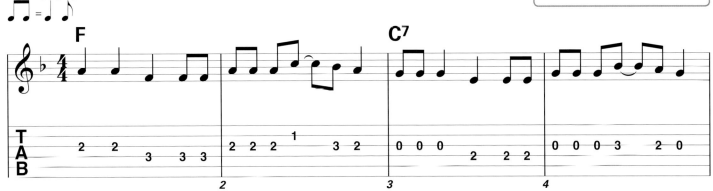

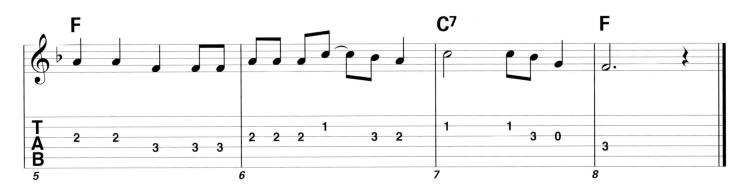

Know your Guitars...
National Reso-lectric

This electric resonator guitar is great for playing the Blues. It has the resonator cone which picks up the acoustic sound and gives the guitar its distinctive tone, as well as an electric pickup so it can be played through an amp. It works equally well for fingerpicking or using a pick. With heavy strings it is extremely suitable for slide playing. By putting lighter strings on this guitar, you can also get great sounds when bending notes.

Guitar Effects…

Overdrive and Distortion

One of the great sounds you can make with an electric guitar and an amp is overdrive (or distortion). This is usually achieved with the help of a pedal which you plug into on the way to the amp. The one shown here is an Ibanez Tube Screamer. There are many distortion pedals available with names like Metal Zone, Super Distortion and Fuzz Box. Try some out at a music store.

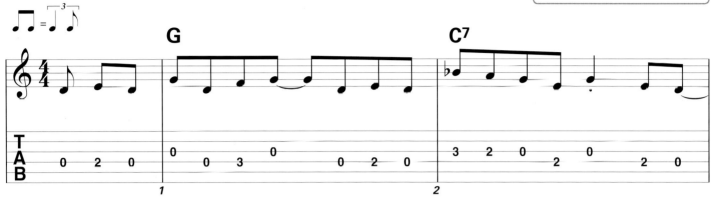

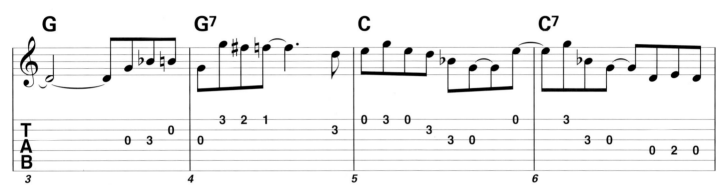

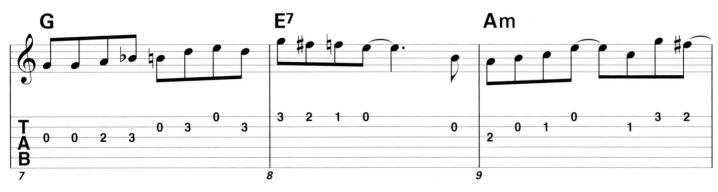

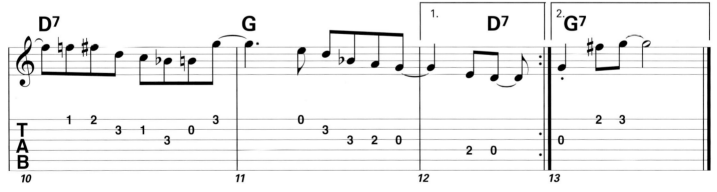

LESSON THIRTY-FIVE

Sixteenth Notes

This is a **sixteenth note**.
It lasts for **one quarter** of a beat.
There are **four** sixteenth notes in one beat.
There are **16** sixteenth notes in one bar of $\frac{4}{4}$ time.

Two sixteenth notes joined together.

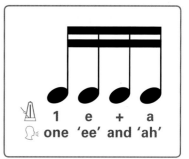

Four sixteenth notes joined together.

▶ 74.0

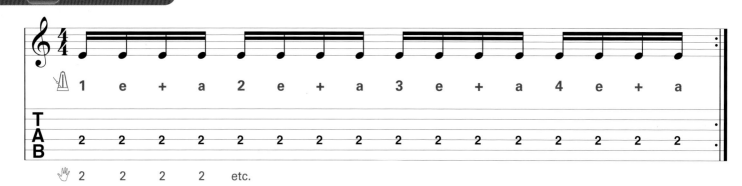

Here is a melody featuring the use of sixteenth notes. Take it slowly at first and count as you play. Tap your foot on each beat and remember that there are four sixteenth notes per beat.

▶ 74.1

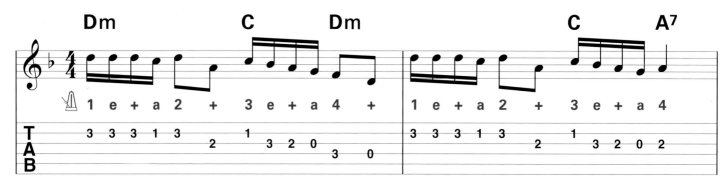

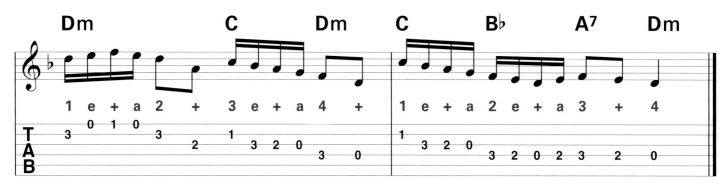

When sixteenth notes are played in conjunction with eighth notes the following timing combinations occur.
An easy way to remember these combinations is that they have the same timing as saying the words chucka-boom and boom-chucka.

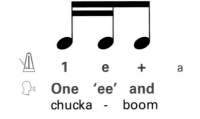

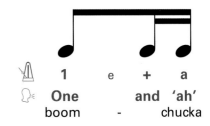

75   Arkansas Traveller

Here is Arkansas Traveller again.
This time it is written in eighth and sixteeenth notes.

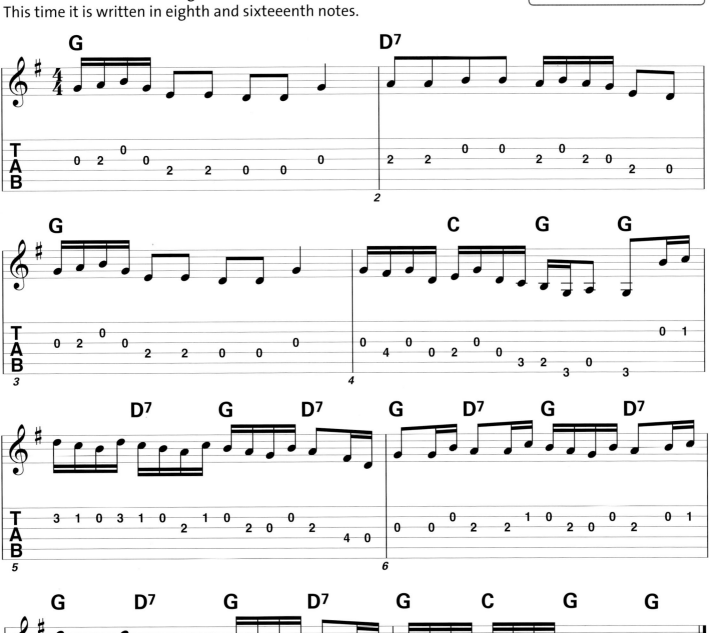

There is often more than one way of writing a rhythm. The next two examples contain similar rhythms, but the first one uses eighth notes while the second uses sixteenth notes. The main difference is where the beats occur. Listen to the recording to hear the different effect produced by these rhythms.

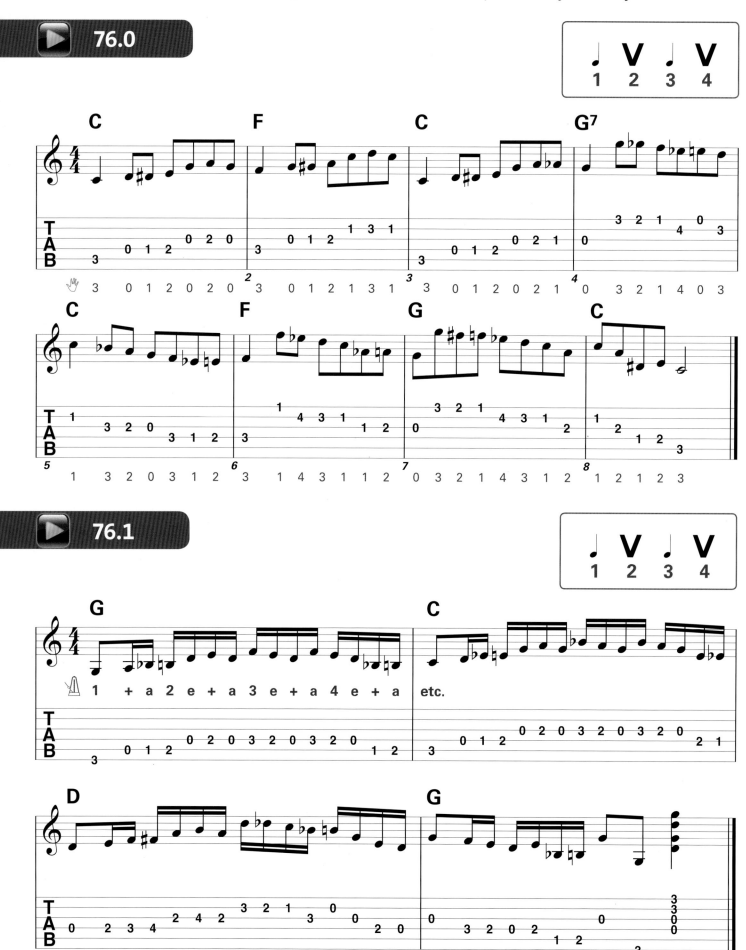

LESSON THIRTY-SIX

Sixteenth Note Rhythms

In Lesson Fifteen you were introduced to eighth note rhythm patterns.

Eighth note strums

In eighth note rhythm patterns there are **2** eighth note strums per beat and **8** eighth note strums in one bar of $\frac{4}{4}$ time. The strum on the '+' count is an up strum.

In **sixteenth note** rhythm patterns there are **4** strums per beat.

 77.0

Play these sixteenth note strums holding an **E** chord.

Sixteenth note strums

There are **4** sixteenth note strums per beat.
There are **16** sixteenth note strums in one bar of $\frac{4}{4}$ time.
Play the **first** down strum of each group of four strums louder, this will help you keep time and make the sixteenth note rhythm easier to play. When playing a sixteenth note rhythm the strum on the '+' count is a down strum.

The following sixteenth note rhythm pattern has sixteenth note strums on the third beat only. Play this pattern holding an **E** chord.

 77.1

Sixteenth note Rhythm Pattern

77.2

Now try a chord progression using this rhythm pattern.

| A | D | A | E |

77.3

This chord progression uses a rhythm pattern with sixteenth notes on the first two beats.

V ∧ V ∧ V ∧ V ∧ V   V
1 e + a 2 e + a 3   4

| Am | G | F | E⁷ |

Here are some sixteenth note rhythm patterns. Practice them holding an **E** chord and then apply them to any chord progression. These patterns combine sixteenth note strums with quarter note strums.

77.4

V ∧ V ∧ V   V   V
1 e + a 2   3   4

77.5

V ∧ V ∧ V   V ∧ V ∧ V
1 e + a 2   3 e + a 4

77.6

V   V ∧ V ∧ V   V ∧ V ∧
1   2 e + a 3   4 e + a

77.7

V   V ∧ V ∧ V ∧ V ∧ V ∧ V ∧
1   2 e + a 3 e + a 4 e + a

The following chord progression uses a rhythm pattern which combines eighth note strums and sixteenth note strums. Notice that the eighth note strums on the '+' count is a down strum. When playing eighth note strums in conjunction with sixteenth note strums, the eighth note strum is a down strum (unlike the eighth note strums in an eighth note rhythm pattern where they are played as an up-strum. See page 65).

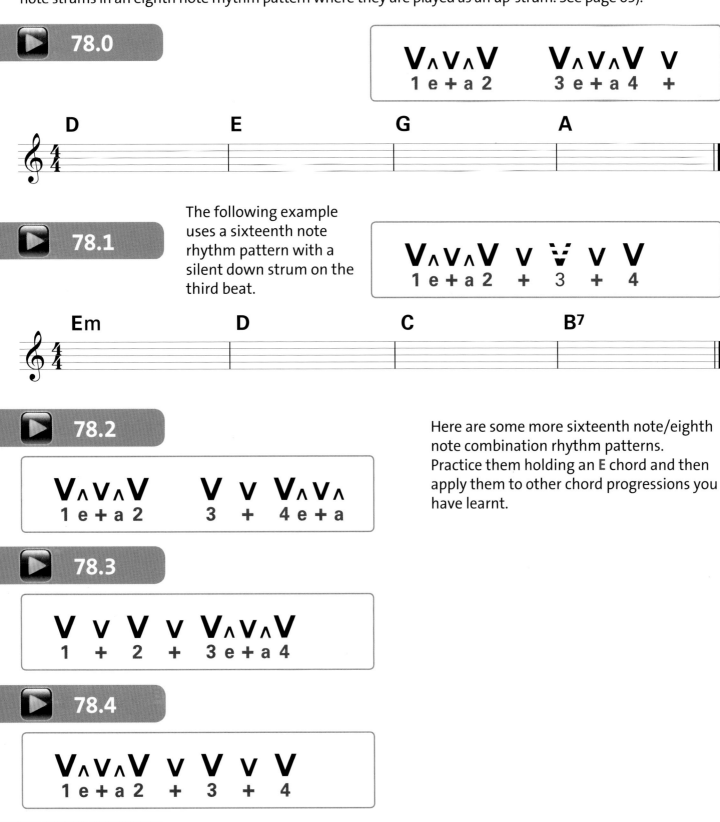

The following example uses a sixteenth note rhythm pattern with a silent down strum on the third beat.

Here are some more sixteenth note/eighth note combination rhythm patterns. Practice them holding an **E** chord and then apply them to other chord progressions you have learnt.

Major Seventh Chords

Another chord type you will need to know is the **major seventh**. The major seventh chord symbol is **maj7**. Here are the six most common open chord shapes for **maj7** chords.

Cmaj7

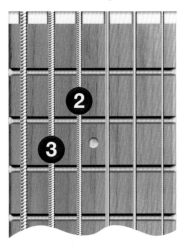

C Major Seventh Chord

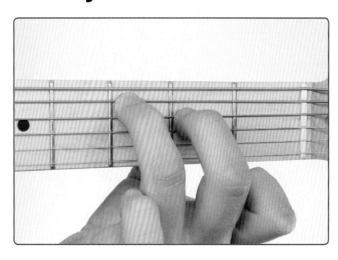

Cmaj7

To play the **Cmaj7** chord, strum all **six** strings. Notice that the **Cmaj7** chord shape is just a **C** chord shape with the **first** finger lifted off.

 79.0

```
V       V       VᴧVᴧV
1       2       3 e + a 4
```

The following chord progression contains the **C major seventh** chord and uses sixteenth note strums in the third beat of the rhythm pattern. Use pivot fingers when changing between **Cmaj7** to **Am** and **F** to **G7**

| Cmaj⁷ | Am | F | G⁷ |

Fmaj7

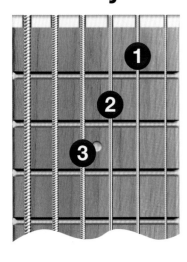

F Major Seventh Chord

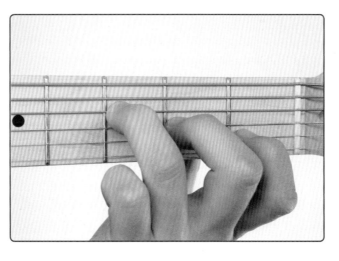

Fmaj7

To play the **Fmaj7** chord, strum all **six** strings. The **Fmaj7** chord shape is just an **F** chord without the F note on the **1st** string.

79.1

The following chord progression contains **Fmaj7** chords and uses sixteenth note rhythm pattern 11. Use a pivot finger when changing between **Fmaj7** and **Dm**.

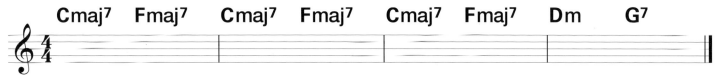

Dotted Eighth Notes

Another common sixteenth note timing is when a sixteenth note is played after a dotted eighth note, i.e.

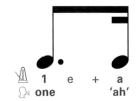

The dot placed after the eighth note lengthens the note by half its value. The dotted eighth note is equivalent to the duration of three sixteenth notes, i.e.

 80   Light and Breezy

This melody contains dotted eighth notes and is accompanied by the same chords as the previous example.

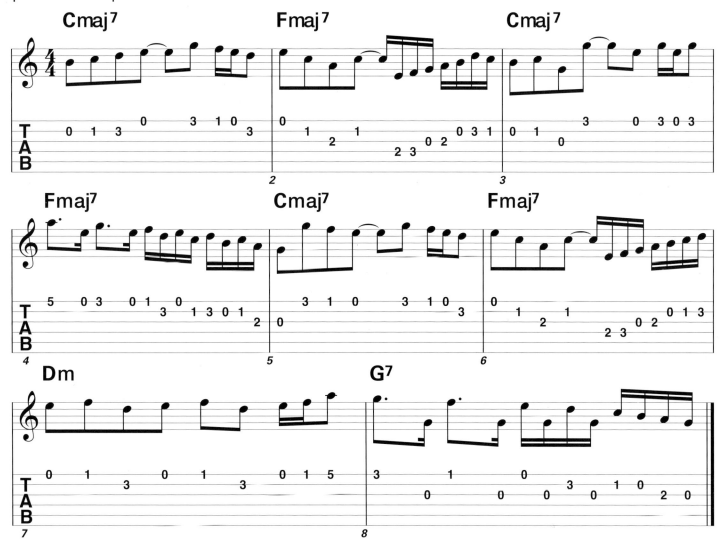

G Major Seventh Chord

Gmaj7

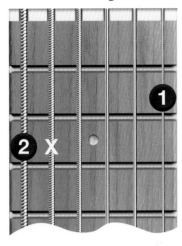

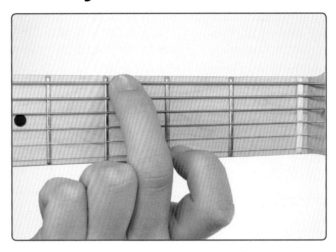

Gmaj7

Strum all **six** strings to play this **Gmaj7** chord shape. The **X** above the **5th** string indicates that note is not in the chord and is deadened. In this chord shape the **second** finger of the left hand lightly touches the **5th** string, which deadens it, so even when you strum the **5th** string it makes no sound.

 81.0

Apply sixteenth note rhythm pattern 8 to the following chord progression. Practice the chord progression using an easy rhythm pattern before using the suggested pattern.

V∧V∧V V V̌ V V
1 e + a 2 + 3 + 4

| Gmaj⁷ | Cmaj⁷ | Fmaj⁷ | Dm | Cmaj⁷ |

A Major Seventh Chord

Amaj7

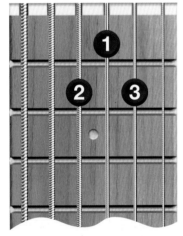

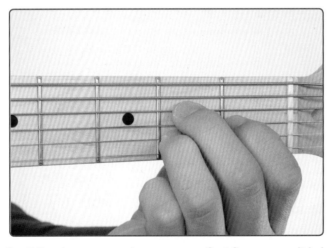

Amaj7

Strum all **six** strings. The **Amaj7** chord shape is an **A** chord shape with the **first** finger playing the **first** fret instead of the **second** fret.

 81.1

In the following progression, use your first finger as a slide between all chord changes. The first finger does not lose contact with the 3rd string throughout the entire progression. The two bar rhythm pattern combines quarter, eighth, sixteenth, and silent strums.

V V V∧V∧V   V∧V∧V V V̌ V V
1 2 3 e + a 4   1 e + a 2 + 3 + 4
——First Bar——   ——Second Bar——

| A | Amaj⁷ | D | E⁷ |

Dmaj7

D Major Seventh Chord

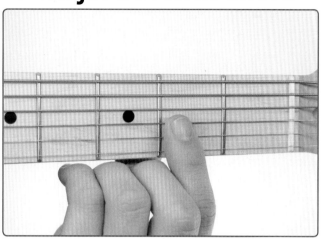

Dmaj7

Strum only **five** strings. Use the **first** finger to **bar** all three notes on the **1st**, **2nd** and **3rd** strings of the **second** fret.

Change chords with an up strum on the 'and' section of the second beat

V ∧ V ∧ V ∧ V
1 + 2 + 3 + 4

▶ 81.2

Practice the chord changes with an easy rhythm pattern before using the suggested rhythm pattern.

D	Dmaj⁷	Gmaj⁷	A⁷

Emaj7

E Major Seventh Chord

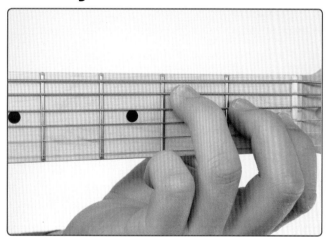

Emaj7

Strum all **six** strings. The **Emaj7** chord shape is the same as the **E** chord shape except for the note on the 4th string.

The following chord progression contains all the major seventh chord shapes learnt in this lesson. Practice this progression with an easy strum pattern first. Once you are confident with the chord changes, use the suggested rhythm pattern.

▶ 81.3

Change chords on this strum

V ∧ V ∧ V   V   V   V   V
1 e + a 2   +   3   +   4

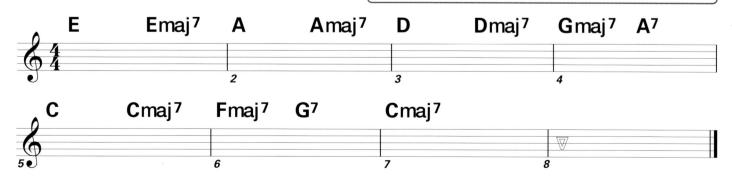

LESSON THIRTY-EIGHT

Minor Seventh Chords

Another chord type you will need to know is the **minor seventh**. The minor seventh chord symbol is **m7**. Here are the most common open chord shapes for **m7** chords.

Dm7

D Minor Seventh Chord

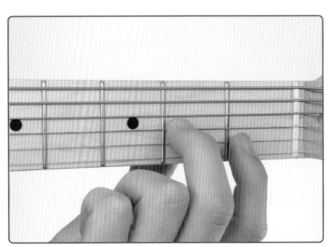

▶ 82.0

Dm7

Strum only **five** strings. Use the **first** finger to **bar** across the **1st** and **2nd** strings at the **first** fret. The **Dm7** chord is easier to play if you position your second finger before positioning your first finger.

V	v	V	v	V̌	v	V	V	∧	v	∧	V	v	V̌	v	V
1	+	2	+	3	+	4	1	e	+	a	2	+	3	+	4

Cmaj⁷   Am   Dm⁷   G⁷

$\frac{4}{4}$

Am7

A Minor Seventh Chord

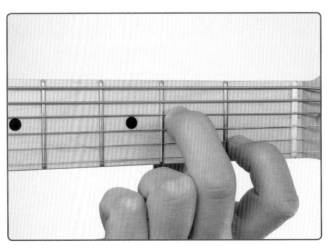

Am7

Strum all **six** strings. The **Am7** chord shape is an **Am** chord shape with the **third** finger lifted off.

82.1

V∧V∧V V V∧V∧V
1 e + a 2 + 3 e + a 4

Dm⁷	G⁷	Cmaj⁷	Fmaj⁷	Dm⁷	E⁷	Am⁷	A⁷

Em7

E Minor Seventh Chord

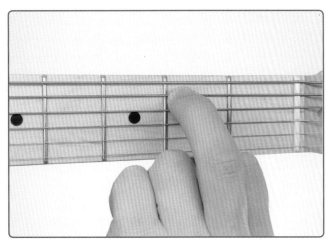

Em7

Strum all **six** strings. This **Em7** shape is like an **Em** shape with the **third** finger lifted off.

82.2

V∧V∧V∧V
1 + 2 + 3 + 4

Use a pivot finger when changing between **Am7** and **D7**.

Gmaj⁷	Em⁷	Am⁷	D⁷

Guitar Setups…
Pickup Combinations

The electric guitars of the 1950's and 60's traditionally had either single coil pickups or humbuckers. Although both companies had exceptions, Fender guitars like the Stratocaster and Telecaster usually had single coil pickups, while Gibson guitars like the Les Paul and the 335 had humbuckers. In the 1970's people began to experiment with both types of pickups on the same guitar. Today there are many guitar manufacturers using the single, single, humbucker combination shown here, making the guitar far more versatile.

As discussed in Lesson Nine there can be more than one way to play a chord. Written below are commonly used alternative chord shapes for the Em7 and Am7 chords. Certain chord shapes sound better or are easier to play depending on the chord progression.

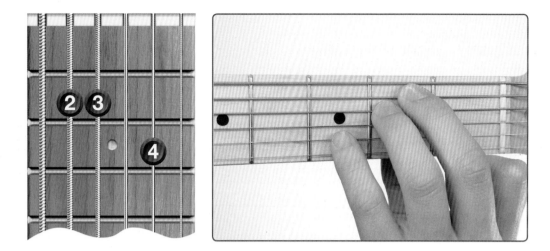

This **Em7** shape is an **Em** chord with an additional note played by the fourth finger.

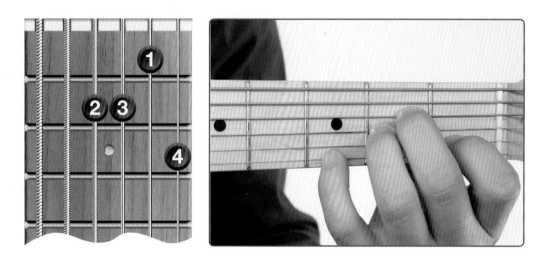

This **Am7** shape is an **Am** chord with an additional note played by the fourth finger.

Use these alternative shapes in the chord progression below.

Use your first finger as a pivot when changing between **Am7** and **D7**.

Here is a melody accompanied by major, minor and dominant 7ths. Notice the symbol indicating that the eighth notes in the melody are played with a swing rhythm. Make sure you play the first and second endings as indicated.

This piece introduces the Bm7(♭5) chord in bar 5. The fingering for this chord is shown on the right.

Bm7(♭5)

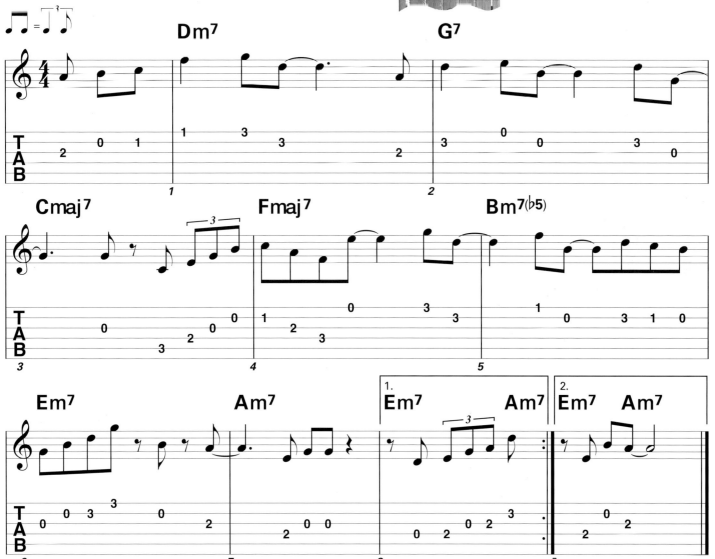

Know your Guitars...
Rickenbacker 12 String

The electric guitar was invented by Adolf Rickenbacker in the 1930's. Rickenbacker guitars are now commonly used in Rock and Pop music. The Rickenbacker 12 string was made famous by George Harrison of the Beatles. It is also used by Roger McGuinn of the Byrds and by Tom Petty. 12 string guitars contain six courses of two strings side by side, with the two strings tuned an octave apart. The 12 string has a singing quality and is great for both chords and picking melodies.

LESSON THIRTY-NINE

The next chord progression contains a new chord, **D6**.

D6

D Sixth Chord

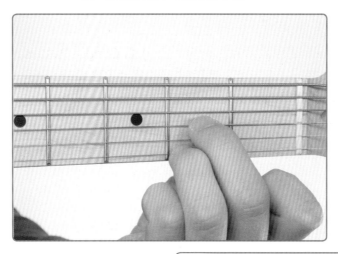

84.0

D6

Strum only **five** strings. The chord shape given uses the **second** and **third** fingers. You could use your **first** and **second** fingers as an alternative fingering.

Em⁷	A⁷	Dmaj⁷	D⁶	D

Another commonly used sixth chord shape is **G6**.

G6

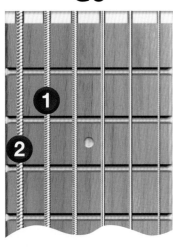

G Sixth Chord

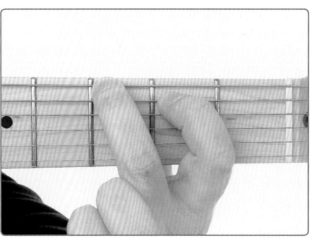

84.1

G6

The **G6** chord shape is like a **G** chord with the **third** finger lifted off.

D	Dmaj⁷	D⁶	Dmaj⁷	D	Dmaj⁷	D⁶	Dmaj⁷

152   PROGRESSIVE GUITAR

www.learntoplaymusic.com

Another common key for guitar is the key of **E minor (Em)**. El Condor Pasa is in the key of E minor and uses notes from the E minor scale. The key signature for E minor is the same as G major, that is it contains one sharp, **F sharp (F♯)**. It is common for songs in the key of E minor to contain a **D sharp (D♯)** in the melody.

Tempo Markings

The term **tempo** refers to the **speed** at which music is played. Tempo markings come from Italian words. Some of them are listed below, along with their English translations. It is important to be able to recognize these markings and to be able to play comfortably at each tempo.

Adagio slowly   **Andante** an easy walking pace   **Moderato** a moderate speed

Allegro fast   **Presto** very fast

86   Hasta la Vista

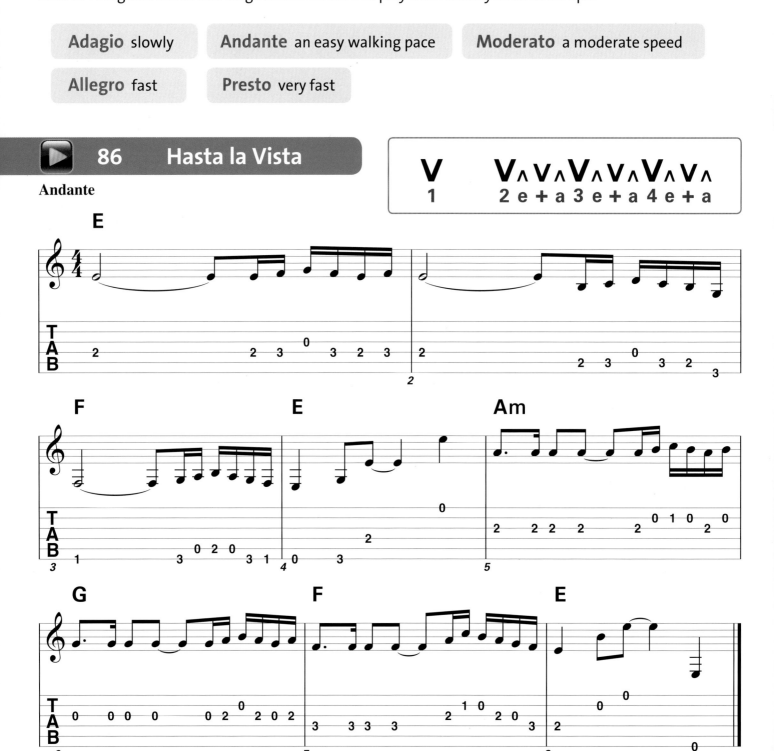

The Two Four Time Signature

The $\frac{2}{4}$ time signature tells you that there are only two quarter note beats in one bar. The only difference between $\frac{2}{4}$ and $\frac{4}{4}$ is that in $\frac{2}{4}$ time there are twice as many bar lines.

When playing 2 chords per bar, use the second rhythm pattern.

87   Dixie

LESSON FORTY

Cut Common Time

The following solo is in **Cut Common time**. The time signature is similar to that of Common time ($\frac{4}{4}$), but has a vertical line through it ¢. It is also called $\frac{2}{2}$ time and represents two half note beats per bar. In this situation, each half note receives one count. Whole notes receive two counts, while quarter notes receive half a count. Some of the notes are further up the fretboard than you have played previously. The positions of these notes can be found in the Tab.

Notice also the frequent use of chromatic notes in this solo.

88   Bluegrass Junction

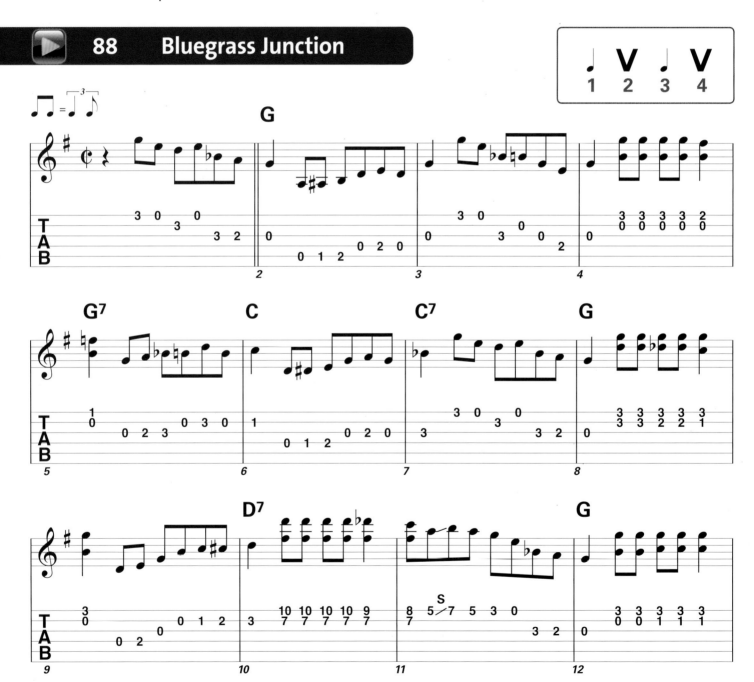

www.learntoplaymusic.com

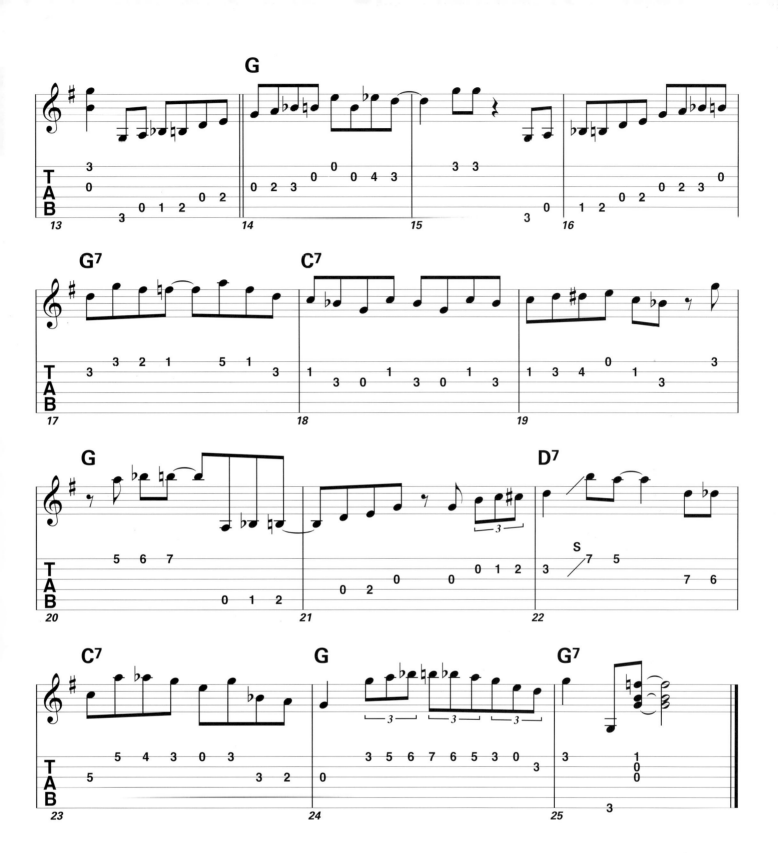

Supplementary Songs

Try accompanying this song with a rock chord accompaniment using a shuffle rhythm.

89   Triplet Trip

This piece is quite challenging, so take it slowly at first. The high B♭ note in bars 7 and 11 is at the 6th fret on the first string and is played by the 4th finger.
You will notice in bar 4 and 7 that an Fsus chord and an Em7(♭5) are introduced respectively.
These chords can both be found in the chord chart in Appendix Three.

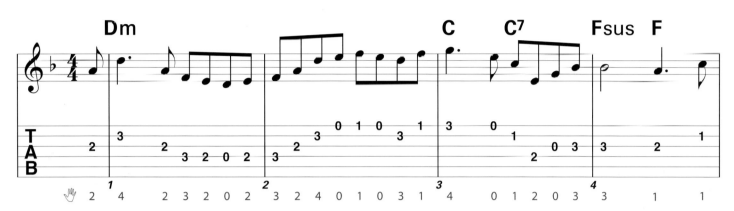

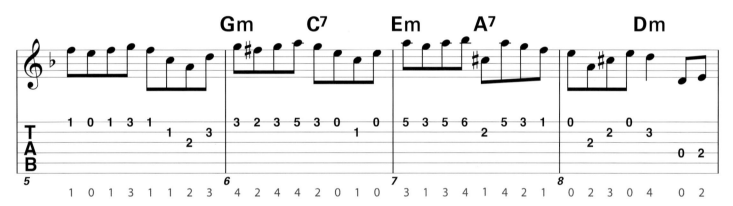

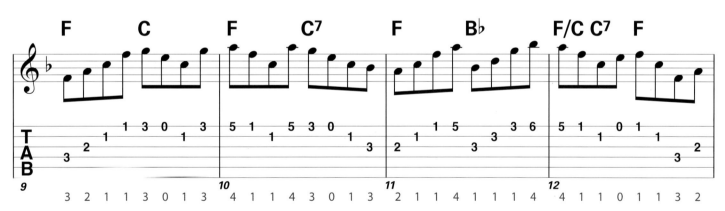

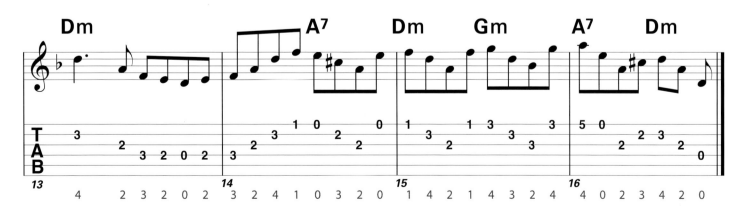

The fingering of the **F#dim** chord in bar 30 uses the same fingering as the Cdim chord learned page 120. These diminished chord shapes can be moved 3 frets up or down the fretboards and it will still retain the same chord name, the notes just appear in a different order. In this example, the F#dim chord is fingered at the fourth fret.

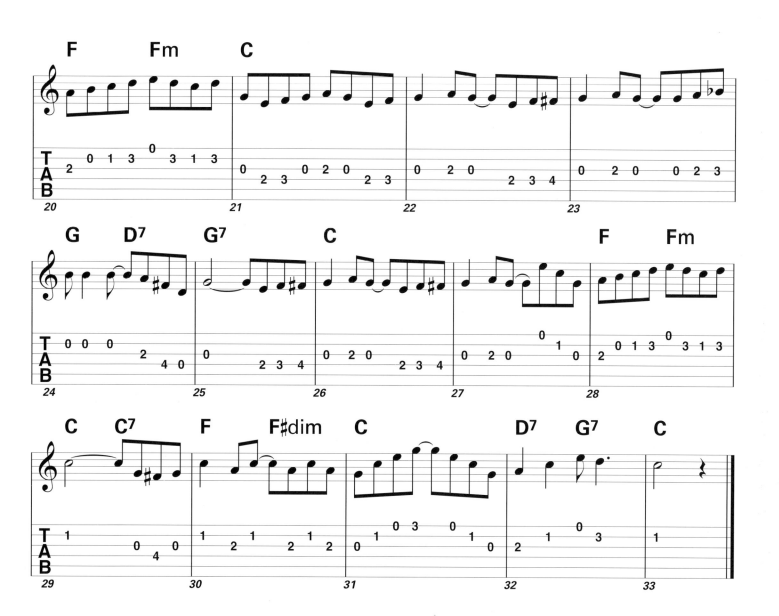

Electric Guitar Pickups...
Single Coil Pickups

Electric guitars contain pickups which capture the sound coming from the strings and send the signal to the amplifier. The original pickups were single coil pickups similar to the one shown here. These pickups are commonly found in Fender guitars like the Stratocaster which contains three single coil pickups, and the Telecaster which contains two different single coil pickups.

92   Tell It Like It Is

Notice on the recording the strumming changes in the last two bars, mimicking the rhythm of the lead part instead of playing rhythm pattern. This is done to make the song sound finished.

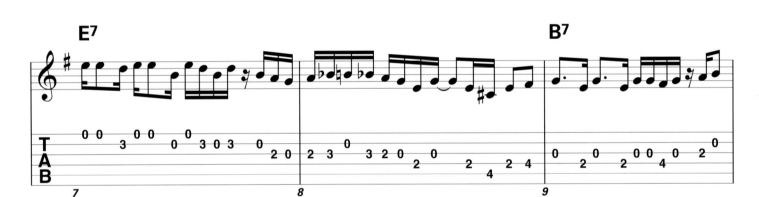

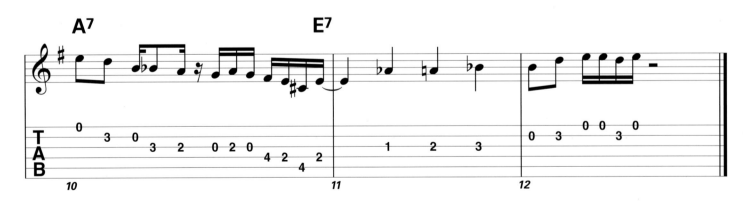

APPENDICES

APPENDIX ONE	Tuning
APPENDIX TWO	Notes on the Guitar Fretboard Keys and Scales
APPENDIX THREE	Chord Charts Song List
APPENDIX FOUR	Transposing
APPENDIX FIVE	Playing in a Band
APPENDIX SIX	Chord Formula Chart Glossary of Musical Terms

Appendix One - Tuning

It is essential for your guitar to be in tune, so that the chords and notes you play will sound correct. The main problem with tuning for most beginning students is that the ear is not able to determine slight differences in pitch. For this reason you should seek the aid of a teacher or an experienced guitarists. Several methods can be used to tune the guitar. These include:

1. Tuning to another musical instrument (e.g. piano, guitar or another guitar).
2. Tuning to pitch pipes or a tuning fork
3. Tuning the guitar to itself.
4. Using an electronic tuner.

The most common and useful of these is tuning the guitar to itself. This method involves finding notes of the same pitch on different strings. The adjacent diagram outlines the notes used:

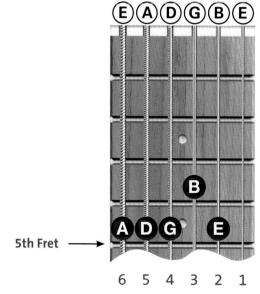

5th Fret →

6 5 4 3 2 1

The method of tuning is as follows:

1. Tune the open sixth string to either:
    (a) The open sixth string of another guitar.
    (b) A piano.

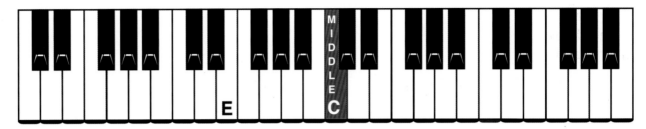

The piano key equivalent to the open 6th string is indicated on the diagram above.

(c) Pitch pipes, which produce notes that correspond with each of the 6 open strings.

(d) A tuning fork. Most tuning forks give the note A.

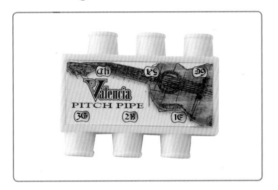

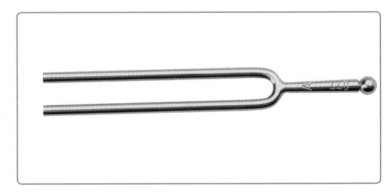

To produce sound from the tuning fork, hold it by the stem and tap one of the prongs against something hard. This will set up a vibration, which can be heard clearly when the bass of the stem is then placed on a solid surface, e.g. a guitar body.

2. Place a finger on the 6th string at the fifth fret. Now play the open A (5th string). If the guitar is to be in tune, then these two notes must have the same pitch (i.e. sound the same). If they do not sound the same, the 5th string must be adjusted to match the note produced on the 6th string, i.e. it is tuned in relation to the 6th string.

3. Tune the open 4th string to the note on the fifth fret of the 5th string, using the method outlined above.

4. Tune all other strings using the same procedure, remembering that the open B string (2nd) is tuned to the 4th fret (check diagram) while all other strings are tuned to the 5th fret.

5. Strum an open E major chord, to check if your guitar is tuned correctly. At first may have some difficulty deciding whether or not the chord sound is correct, but as your ear improves you will become more familiar with the correct sound of the chord.

Tuning may take you many months to master, and you should practice it constantly. The guidance of a teacher will be an invaluable aid in the early stages of guitar tuning.

Tuning Hints

One of the easiest ways to practice tuning is to actually start with the guitar in tune and then de-tune one string. When you do this, always take the string **down** in pitch (i.e. loosen it) as it is easier to tune "up" to a given note rather than "down" to it. As an example, de-tune the 4th string (D). If you strum a chord now, the guitar will sound out of tune, even though only one string has been altered (so remember that if your guitar is out of tune it may only be one string at fault).

Following the correct method, you must tune the 4th string against the D note at the fifth fret of the 5th string. Play the note loudly, and listen carefully to the sound produced. This will help you retain the correct pitch in your mind when tuning the next string.

Now that you have listened carefully to the note that you want, the D string must be tuned to it. Play the D string, and turn its tuning key at the same time, and you will hear the pitch of the string change (it will become higher as the tuning key tightens the string). It is important to follow this procedure, so that you hear the sound of the string at all times, as it tightens. You should also constantly refer back to the correct sound that is required (i.e. the D note on the fifth fret of the 5th string).

Electronic Tuners

Electronic tuners make tuning your guitar very easy. They allow you to tune each string individually to the tuner, by indicating whether the notes are sharp (too high) or flat (too low). It is still recommended however, that you practice tuning your guitar by the above method to help improve your musicianship.

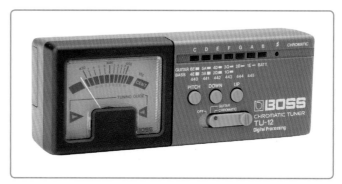

Electronic Tuner

Tuning Your Guitar to the CD or DVD

The DVDs, DVD-ROM and CD contain recordings of the open strings of a guitar. Each string is played several times, giving you sufficient time to tune the corresponding string on your guitar to the sound of the note on the recording. You may also be able to program your player to repeat a specific track several times, increasing the amount of times the note can be heard. The recording contains open string tuning notes for steel string acoustic and electric guitars. Beginners may find it easier to tune the strings of their guitar to the corresponding type of guitar on the recording. Each type of guitar has its own particular tonal characteristics and first time tuners will be able to hear the sound of a string that best matches the sound of their instrument. As with all tuning methods, make sure you practice tuning to the recording in a quiet environment and double check that you are adjusting the correct tuning key before turning.

Appendix Two - Notes on the Guitar Fretboard

Notes in the Open Position

The **open position** of the guitar contains the notes of the open strings and the first three frets. Outlined below are the position of these notes on the staff, Tab, and on the fretboard. Also shown is an example of two separate **octaves**, an octave being two notes that have the same letter name and are eight consecutive notes apart. All the songs and examples in this book use notes in the open position.

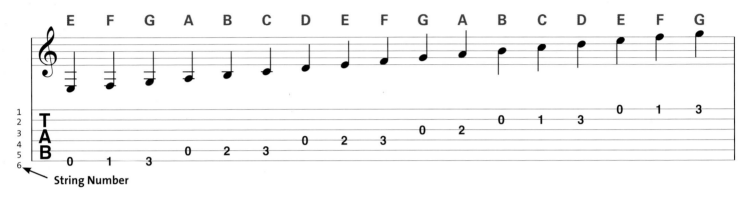

Sharps and Flats

A **sharp** (♯) raises the pitch of a note by one semitone (1 fret). A **flat** (♭) lowers the pitch of a note by one semitone. In music notation the ♯ and ♭ signs are placed before the note on the staff.

Notes on the

Here is a fretboard diagram of all the notes on the guitar. Play the notes on each string the open note. For example the open 6th string is an **E** note and the note on the 12th

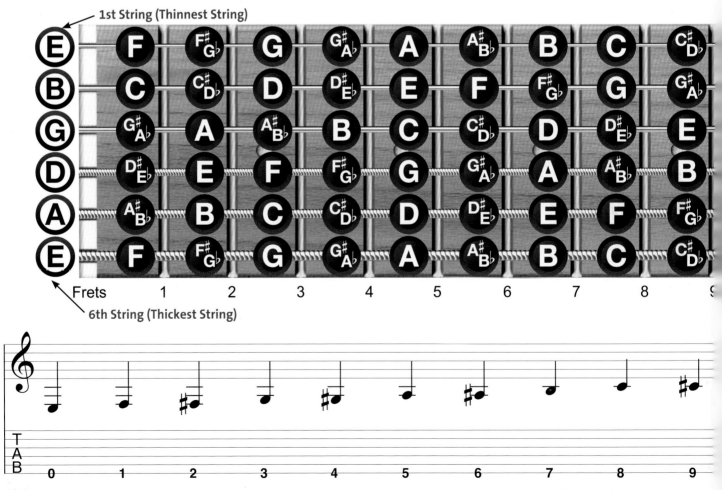

www.learntoplaymusic.com

The Chromatic Scale

With the inclusion of sharps and flats, there are 12 different notes within one octave as shown below. The notes **EF** and **BC** are always on semitone apart (1 fret). The other notes are a tone apart (2 frets). Sharps (♯) and flats (♭) are found between the notes that are a tone apart:

This scale is called the **chromatic scale** and contains all the sharps (♯'s) and flats (♭'s) possible. **C sharp (C♯)** has the same position on the fretboard as **D flat (D♭)**. They are the same note but can have different names depending upon what key you are playing in. The same applies to D♯/E♭, F♯/G♭, G♯/A♭ and A♯/B♭. These are called **enharmonic notes**. Written below are all the notes on the **guitar** including these sharps and flats.

Also notice that:
The **5th fret of the 6th string** (A note) is the same note as the **open 5th string**.
The **5th fret of the 5th string** (D note) is the same note as the **open 4th string**.
The **5th fret of the 4th string** (G note) is the same note as the **open 3rd string**.
The **4th fret of the 3rd string** (B note) is the same note as the **open 2nd string**.
The **5th fret of the 2nd string** (E note) is the same note as the **open 1st string**.

These note positions are important to remember because they are the basis for tuning your guitar to itself (see **Appendix 1**). All the notes on each of the six strings are shown on the fretboard diagram below. All the notes on the 6th string have been notated on a music staff and TAB below the fretboard diagram.

Guitar Fretboard

from the open notes to the 12th fret. The note on the 12th fret is one octave higher than fret of the 6th string is also an **E** note, but is one octave higher.

Learning all the Keys

The term "**key**" describes the central note around which a piece of music is based. For example a piece of music in the key of **C** would derive its notes and chords from a **C major scale**. A piece of music in the key of **A** would derive its notes and chords from the **A major scale**, and so on. After you have learnt a scale or mode in one key, it is a good idea to practice playing in every key. **E** and **A** are fairly common keys for guitar, but if you are playing with a singer, you would have to play in whatever key suits their particular voice. That could be $F\sharp$ or $D\flat$ for example. Piano players tend to like the keys of **C**, **F** and **G**, and horn players like flat keys such as **F**, $B\flat$ and $E\flat$. So, you can see there are good reasons for learning to play equally well in every key.

A good way to learn to play in all keys is to use the **key cycle** (also called the cycle of 5ths or cycle of 4ths). It contains the names of all the keys and is fairly easy to memorise.

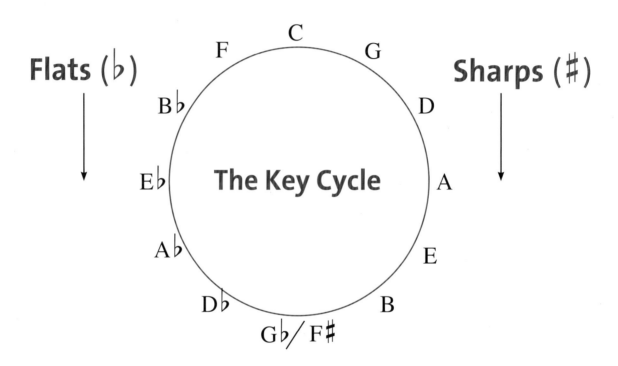

Think of the key cycle like a clock. Just as there are 12 points on the clock, there are also 12 keys. **C** is at the top and it contains no sharps or flats. Moving around clockwise you will find the next key is **G**, which contains one sharp ($F\sharp$). The next key is **D**, which contains two sharps ($F\sharp$ and $C\sharp$). Progressing further through the sharp keys each key contains an extra sharp, with the new sharp being the 7th note of the new key, the other sharps being any which were contained in the previous key. Therefore the key of A would automatically contain $F\sharp$ and $C\sharp$ which were in the key of D, plus $G\sharp$ which is the 7th note of the A major scale. As you progress around the cycle, each key introduces a new sharp. When you get to $F\sharp$ (at 6 o'clock), the new sharp is called $E\sharp$ which is enharmonically the same as **F**. **Enharmonic** means two different ways of writing the same note. Another example of enharmonic spelling would be $F\sharp$ and $G\flat$. This means that $G\flat$ could become the name of the key of $F\sharp$. The key of $F\sharp$ contains six sharps, while the key of $G\flat$ contains six flats.

If you start at **C** again at the top of the cycle and go anti-clockwise you will progress through the flat keys. The key of **F** contains one flat ($B\flat$), which then becomes the name of the next key around the cycle. In flat keys, the new flat is always the 4th degree of the new key. Continuing around the cycle, the key of $B\flat$ contains two flats ($B\flat$ and $E\flat$) and so on.

Key Signatures

When a song or chord progression is said to be in a particular key it means that the melody or chords used are based upon a particular major or minor scale. As mentioned on the previous page, a song or chord progression in the key of A major would contain a melody which uses note from the A major scale. The key of a melody line is indicated by the **key signature**, which indicates which major or minor scale the song uses. Listed below are the key signatures for each major key and its relative minor key. The notes in the relative minor scale are the same as the notes in the major scale, except that they start and end on different notes. For example the C major and A minor scales contain the same notes and therefore have the same key signature. A minor is the relative minor to C major.

KEY SIGNATURE	MAJOR KEY MOST COMMON CHORDS	RELATIVE MINOR KEY MOST COMMON CHORDS
	C C, Dm, Em, F, G, Am	**Am** Am, C, Dm, Em, F, G,
	G G, Am, Bm, C, D, Em	**Em** Em, G, Am, Bm, C, D
	D D, Em, F♯m, G, Am Bm	**Bm** Bm, D, Em, F♯m, G, Am
	A A, Bm, C♯m, D, E, F♯m	**F♯m** F♯m, A, Bm, C♯m, D, E
	E E, F♯m, G♯m, A, B, C♯m	**C♯m** C♯m, E, F♯m, G♯m, A, B
	B B, C♯m, D♯m, E, F♯ , G♯m	**G♯m** G♯m, B, C♯m, D♯m, E, F♯
	F♯ F♯, G♯m, A♯m, B, C♯ , D♯m	**D♯m** D♯m F♯, G♯m, A♯m, B, C♯
	F F, Gm, Am, B♭, C, Dm	**Dm** Dm, F, Gm, Am, B♭, C
	B♭ B♭, Cm, Dm, E♭, F, Gm	**Gm** Gm, B♭, Cm, Dm, E♭, F
	E♭ E♭, Fm, Gm, A♭, B♭, Cm	**Cm** Cm, E♭, Fm, Gm, A♭, B♭
	A♭ A♭, B♭m, Cm, D♭, E♭, Fm	**Fm** Fm, A♭, B♭m, Cm, D♭, E♭
	D♭ D♭, E♭m, Fm, G♭, A♭, B♭m	**B♭m** B♭m, D♭, E♭m, Fm, G♭, A♭

Scales

A scale can be defined as a series of notes, in alphabetical order, going from any given note to its octave and based upon some form of set pattern. The pattern upon which most scales are based involves a set sequence of **tones** and/or **semitones**. On the guitar, a tone is two frets and a semitone is one fret. As an example, the **B** note is a tone higher than **A**, (two frets), whereas the **C** note is only a semitone higher than **B** (one fret). Of the other natural notes in music, **E** and **F** are a semitone apart, and all the others are a tone apart.

Natural Notes

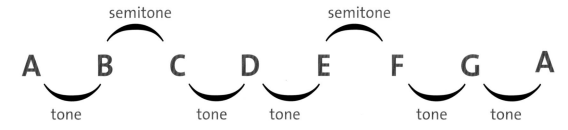

In music theory, a tone may be referred to as a **step** and a semitone as a **half-step**.

The main types of scales that you need to become familiar with are the **chromatic**, **major**, **minor**, **minor pentatonic** and **blues** scales.

The Chromatic Scale

The **chromatic** scale is based upon a sequence of **semitones** only and this includes every possible note within one octave. Here is the **C chromatic scale**.

C   C♯   D   D♯   E   F   F♯   G   G♯   A   A♯   B   C

The same scale could be written out using flats, however it is more common to do this when descending, as such;

C   B   B♭   A   A♭   G   G♭   F   E   E♭   D   D♭   C

Because each chromatic scale contains every possible note within one octave, once you have learnt one you have basically learnt them all. As an example, the **A** chromatic scale (written below) contains exactly the same notes as the **C** chromatic scale, the only difference between them being the note upon which they commence. This starting note, in all scales, is referred to as the **tonic** or **key note**.

The A Chromatic Scale

A   A♯   B   C   C♯   D   D♯   E   F   F♯   G   G♯   A

The Major Scale

The most common scale in Western music is called the **major scale**. This scale is based upon a sequence of both tones and semitones, and is sometimes referred to as a **diatonic** scale. Here is the major scale sequence;

TONE	TONE	SEMITONE	TONE	TONE	TONE	SEMITONE
T	T	S	T	T	T	S

Starting on the **C** note and following through this sequence gives the **C major** scale;

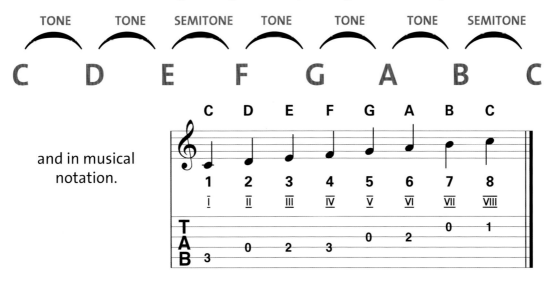

and in musical notation.

Roman numerals are used to number each note of the major scale. Thus **F** is the **fourth** note of the **C major** scale, **G** is the **fifth**, and so on.
The major scale will always give the familiar sound of **DO, RE, MI, FA, SO, LA, TI, DO**.

The major scale **always** uses the same sequence of tones and semitones, no matter what note is used as the tonic. The table below list the 13 most commonly used major scales.

You will notice that, in order to maintain the correct sequence of tones and semitones, all major scales except **C major** involve the use of either sharps or flats. You will notice, when playing these scales, that they all maintain the familiar sound of **DO, RE, MI, FA SO, LA, TI, DO**.

	T	T	S	T	T	T	S
C MAJOR	C	D	E	F	G	A	B	C
G MAJOR	G	A	B	C	D	E	F♯	G
D MAJOR	D	E	F♯	G	A	B	C♯	D
A MAJOR	A	B	C♯	D	E	F♯	G♯	A
E MAJOR	E	F♯	G♯	A	B	C♯	D♯	E
B MAJOR	B	C♯	D♯	E	F♯	G♯	A♯	B
F♯ MAJOR	F♯	G♯	A♯	B	C♯	D♯	E♯	F♯
F MAJOR	F	G	A	B♭	C	D	E	F
B♭ MAJOR	B♭	C	D	E♭	F	G	A	B♭
E♭ MAJOR	E♭	F	G	A♭	B♭	C	D	E♭
A♭ MAJOR	A♭	B♭	C	D♭	E♭	F	G	A♭
D♭ MAJOR	D♭	E♭	F	G♭	A♭	B♭	C	D♭
G♭ MAJOR	G♭	A♭	B♭	C♭	D♭	E♭	F	G♭
Roman Numerals	I	II	III	IV	V	VI	VII	VIII

Minor Keys

In music there are two main types of scales, namely majors and minors. The major scale is based on the following pattern of tones and semitones:

	T		T		S	T		T		T		T		S	
C major	**C**		**D**		**E**	**F**		**G**		**A**		**B**		**C**
	Ī		ĪĪ		ĪĪĪ	ĪV̄		V̄		V̄Ī		V̄ĪĪ		

T - tone
S - semitone

The minor scale is based upon a different pattern of tones and semitones, as outlined in the A minor scale below:

	T		S		T		T		S		T$\frac{1}{2}$		S	
A minor*	A		B		C	D		E		F		G♯		A
	Ī		ĪĪ		ĪĪĪ	ĪV̄		V̄		V̄Ī		V̄ĪĪ		

In minor scale there is a distance of one and a half semitones between the 6th and 7th notes (e.g. in the A minor scale above, F to G).

If you compare the C major and A minor scale, it can be seen that they both contain the same notes, except for the seventh note of the minor scale, which has been sharpened. Because these two scales are so similar, they are called 'relative' scales i.e. A minor is the relative minor scale of C major and vice versa. The same principle is applied to chords; the Am chord is the relative minor of the C chord.

Every major scale has a relative minor, which is based upon the 6th note of the major scale; for example:

	G	**A**	**B**	**C**	**D**	**E**	**F♯**	**G**
G major:	Ī	ĪĪ	ĪĪĪ	ĪV̄	V̄	V̄Ī	V̄ĪĪ	

The E minor scale (the relative minor of G major) will contain the same notes as the G major scale, except for the 7th note (called the leading note) which is sharpened.

	E	**F#**	**G**	**A**	**B**	**C**	**D♯**	**E**
E minor:	Ī	ĪĪ	ĪĪĪ	ĪV̄	V̄	V̄Ī	V̄ĪĪ	

* This minor scale is referred to as the harmonic minor. There are two other types of minor scales, namely the natural (or pure) minor and the melodic minor. These are discussed in more detail in Progressive Lead Guitar.

The following table summarizes the relationship between major and minor keys.

MAJOR KEY	C	Db	D	Eb	E	F	F#	G	Ab	A	Bb	B
RELATIVE MINOR KEY	Am	Bbm	Bm	Cm	C#m	Dm	D#m	Em	Fm	F#m	Gm	G#m

Both the major key and its relative minor share the same key signature, as illustrated in the example below:

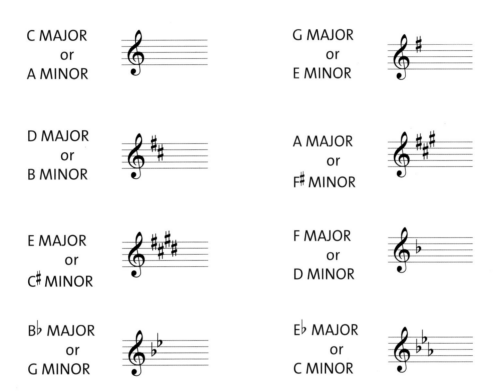

C MAJOR or A MINOR

G MAJOR or E MINOR

D MAJOR or B MINOR

A MAJOR or F# MINOR

E MAJOR or C# MINOR

F MAJOR or D MINOR

Bb MAJOR or G MINOR

Eb MAJOR or C MINOR

The sharpened 7th note that occurs in the relative minor key is never included as part of the key signature. Because each major and relative minor share the same key signature, you will need to know how to distinguish between the two keys. For example if given a piece with the key signature of F# thus:

it could indicate the key of G major, or its relative, E minor. The most accurate way of determining the key is to look through the melody for the sharpened 7th note of the E minor scale (D sharp). The presence of this note will indicate the minor key. If the 7th note is present, but not sharpened, then the key is more likely to be the relative major (i.e. D natural notes would suggest the key of G major).

Another method is to look at the first and last chords of the progression. These chords usually (but not always) indicate the key of the piece. If the piece starts and/or finishes with Em chords then the key is more likely to be E minor.

Appendix Three - Chord Charts

Here is a chart of the types of chords you will most commonly find in sheet music. The shapes given are all based around the first few frets. The other shapes are given for your reference only but in most cases would be better played holding a bar chord shape. Bar chords, although a little difficult at first are ultimately easier and more convenient to play than most of the non-outlined shapes. All good guitarists play bar chords. The boxed shapes are generally easier to play and should be memorised. These open chords sound particularly good on acoustic guitars and for fingerpicking.

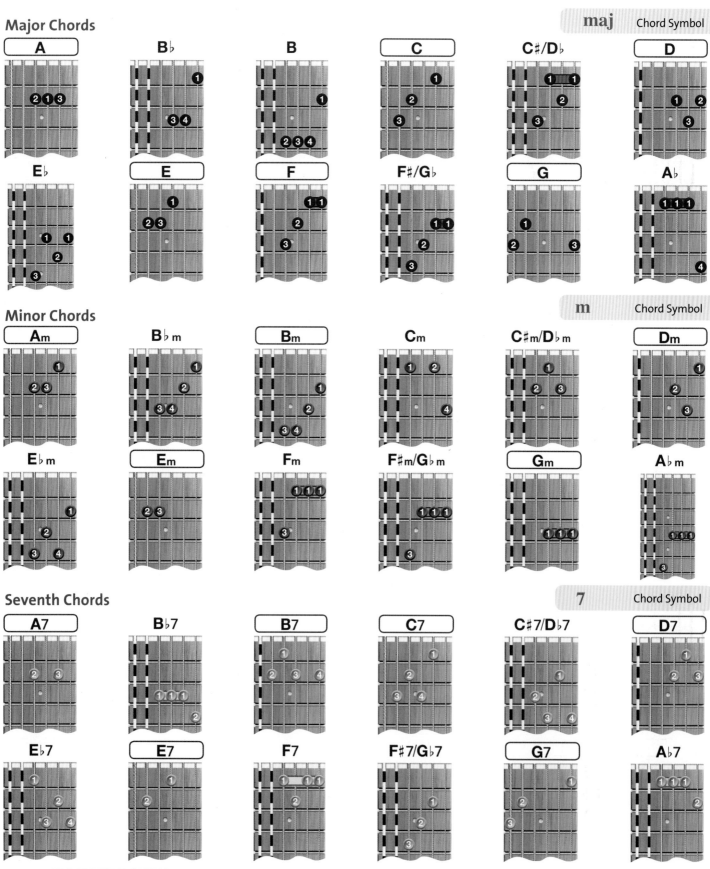

www.learntoplaymusic.com

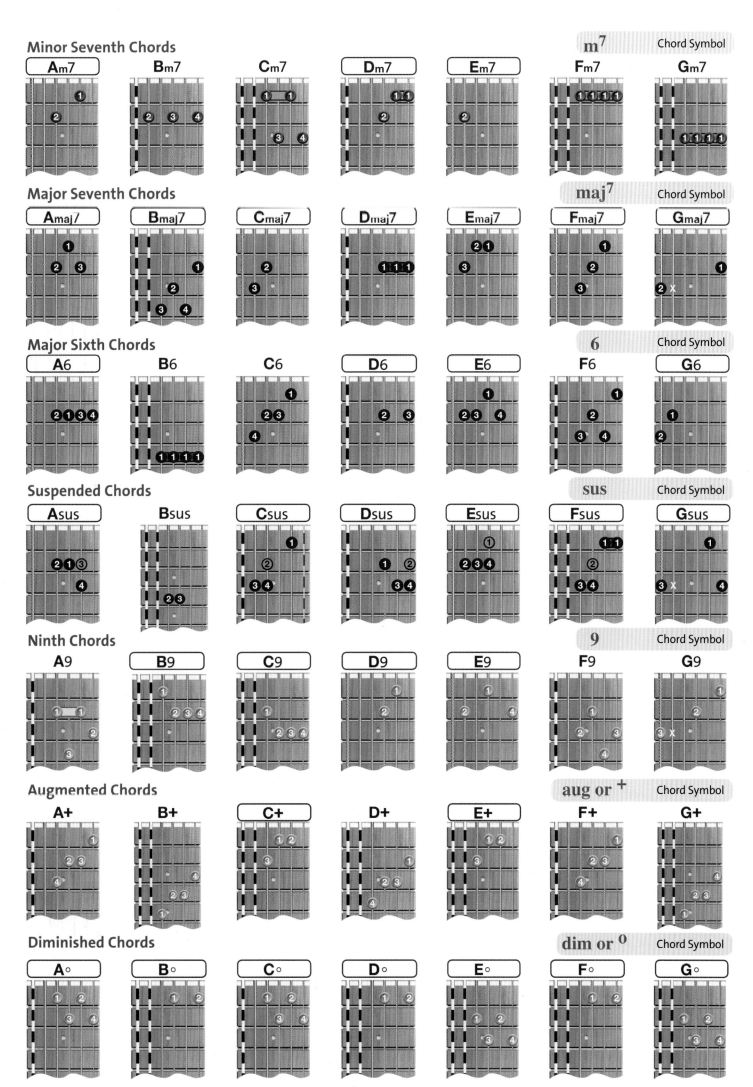

Appendix Three - Song List

In the first section of this book two basic chord progressions are introduced; 12 bar blues and turnarounds (1 and 2). These two progressions are the basis of many songs from the fifties onwards, some of which are listed below.

12 Bar Blues

Be-Bop-A-Lula – Gene Vincent/John Lennon
Hound Dog – Elvis Presley
Johnny B. Goode – Chuck Berry
Boppin' the Blues – Blackfeather
The Wanderer – Dion
Going Up the Country – Canned Heat
Makin' Your Mind Up – Bucks Fizz
Green Door – Shakin' Stevens
In the Summertime – Mungo Jerry
Rock Around the Clock – Bill Haley & His Comets
Barbara Ann – The Beach Boys
Let's Stick Together – Bryan Ferry
Long Tall Glasses (I Know I Can Dance) – Leo Sayer
Blue Suede Shoes – Elvis Presley
School Days (Ring Ring Goes the Bell) – Chuck Berry
Roll Over Beethoven – Chuck Berry
Spirit in the Sky – Norman Greenbaum
Turn Up Your Radio – The Masters Apprentices
Tutti Frutti – Little Richard
Dizzy Miss Lizzie – Larry Williams/The Beatles
Peggy Sue – Buddy Holly
Jailhouse Rock – Elvis Presley
Get Down and Get With It – Slade
Good Golly Miss Molly – Little Richard
Lucille – Little Richard

In the Mood – Glenn Miller
Surfin' Safari – The Beach Boys
Peppermint Twist – Sweet
Boogie Woogie Bugle Boy – The Andrews Sisters/Bette Midler
I Hear You Knockin' – Dave Edmunds
The Boy from New York City – Darts/The Manhattan Transfer
Mountain of Love – Johnny Rivers
I Love to Boogie – T.Rex
Shake Rattle and Roll – Bill Haley & His Comets
Lady Rose – Mungo Jerry
Batman Theme - Nelson Riddle / The Marketts
Spiderman Theme
Stuck in the Middle – Stealers Wheel
Hot Love – T-Rex
The Hucklebuck – Brendan Bowyer
Way Down – Elvis Presley
I Can Help – Billy Swan
Rockin' Robin – Michael Jackson
Red House – Jimi Hendrix
Texas Flood – Stevie Ray Vaughan
Killing Floor – Jimi Hendrix
The Jack – AC/DC
Ice Cream Man - Van Halen
Oh, Pretty Woman – Gary Moore

Turnaround One* (see Lesson 12, page 55).

I Will Always Love You – Whitney Houston
The Night Has a Thousand Eyes – Bobby Vee
It's Raining Again – Supertramp
More – Various Artists
Ti amo – Umberto Tozzi
Crocodile Rock (chorus) – Elton John
One Last Kiss – Various Artists
Stand By Me – John Lennon
Dream – Everly Brothers
Return to Sender – Elvis Presley
Telstar – The Tornadoes
Always Look on the Bright Side of Life – Monty Python
Why do Fools Fall in Love – Frankie Lymon/Diana Ross
Sarah – Fleetwood Mac
Take Good Care of My Baby – Bobby Vee/Smokey
Where Have All the Flowers Gone – Various Artists
Runaround Sue – Dion & the Belmonts
Tell Me Why – The Beatles
Let's Twist Again – Chubby Checker
Stay (Just a Little Bit Longer) – The Four Seasons/
    Jackson Browne
Cool for Cats – UK Squeeze
Y.M.C.A – The Village People
Tired of Toein' the Line – Rocky Burnette
You Drive Me Crazy – Shakin' Stevens
Should I Do It – The Pointer Sisters
Poor Little Fool – Rick Nelson
You Don't Have to Say You Love Me – Dusty Springfield/
Elvis Presley
Breaking Up Is Hard to Do – Neil Sedaka/
The Partridge Family

Oh! Carol – Neil Sedaka
Two Faces Have I – Lou Christie
Every Day – Buddy Hoily
Poetry in Motion – Johnny Tillotson
Happy Birthday, Sweet Sixteen – Neil Sedaka
Big Girls Don't Cry – The Four Seasons
Sherry – The Four Seasons
How Do You Do It? – Gerry & The Pacemakers
Shout, Shout – Rocky Sharp & The Replays
Aces With You – Moon Martin
Houses of the Holy – Led Zeppelin
Uptown Girl – Billy Joel
Build Me Up Buttercup – The Foundations
Happy Days Theme - Pratt & McClain
Joanne – Michael Nesmith
Goodnight Sweetheart – Various Artists
Looking For An Echo – Ol'55
Summer Holiday – Cliff Richard
Be My Baby – The Ronettes/Rachel Sweet
Everlasting Love – Rachel Sweet/Love Affair
I Go To Pieces (verse) – Peter & Gordon
Love Hurts – Everly Brothers/Jim Capaldi/Nazareth
Gee Baby – Peter Shelley
Classic – Adrian Gurvitz
Teenage Dream – T-Rex
Blue Moon – Various Artists
The Tide is High – Blondie
Dennis – Blondie
It Ain't Easy – Normie Rowe
My World – Bee Gees
Hey Paula – Various Artists

It's Only Make Believe – Glen Campbell
Can't Smile Without You – Barry Manilow
Take Good Care of My Baby – Bobby Vee/Smokie
Crossfire – Bellamy Brothers
Bobby's Girl – Marcie Blane
Do That To Me One More Time – Captain & Tenille
Please Mr Postman – Carpenters/ The Beatles
Sharin' The Night Together – Dr Hook
9 to 5 (Morning Train) – Sheena Easton
Diana – Paul Anka
Enola Gay – Orchestral Manoeuvres in the Dark
Some Guys Have All the Luck – Robert Palmer
So Lonely – Get Wet
Hungry Heart – Bruce Springsteen
Land of Make Believe (chorus) – Buck Fizz
Daddys Home – Cliff Richard
The Wonder of You – Elvis Presley
So You Win Again – Hot Chocolate
Hang Five – Rolling Stones
Paper Tiger – Sue Thompson
Venus – Frankie Avalon
Costafine Town – Splinter
If You Leave – OMD
True Blue – Madonna

Turnaround Two

Crocodile Rock (verse) – Elton John	It's A Heatache – Bonnie Tyler	Hurdy Gurdy Man – Donovan
I started a Joke – The Bee Gees	I Don't Like Mondays – The Boomtown Rats	I Go To Pieces (chorus) – Peter & Gordon
Different Drum – Linda Ronstadt	My Angel Baby – Toby Beau	Get It Over With – Angie Gold
Key Largo – Bertie Higgins	Land Of Make Believe (verse) – Bucks Fizz	Sad Sweet Dreamer – Sweet Sensation
Black Berry Way – The Move	I'm In the Mood for Dancing – The Nolans	Down Town – Petula Clark
Georgy Girl – Seekers	What's in a Kiss – Gilbert O'Sullivan	Easy – Oakridge Boys
Where Do You Go To My Lovely – Peter Sarsted	My Baby Loves Love – Joe Jeffries	Only You Can Do It – Francoiose Hardy
Mrs Brown, You've Got a Lovely Daughter – Hermans Hermit	Dreamin' – Johnny Burnett	Costafine – Splinter (chorus)
Toast and Marmalade for Tea – Tin Tin	Cruel To Be Kind – Nick Lowe	Where Did Our Love Go? – Phil Collins
Movie Star – Harpo	Where Did Our Love Go – Diana Ross & The Supremes	

Sheet Music

You should try to work from sheet music as much as possible. Nearly all sheet music is arranged for piano and this presents problems for guitarists. Piano music uses three staves thus:

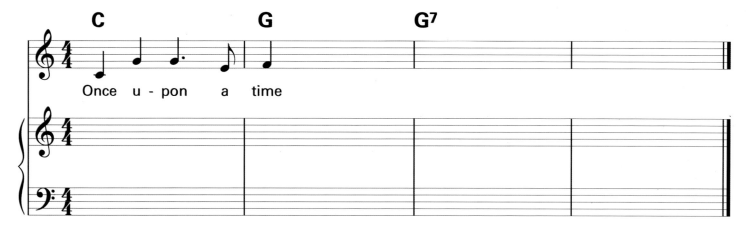

A guitar player need only look at the top stave, which contains the melody line (the tune), the lyrics and the chords. Sheet music does not indicate what rhythm the guitarist should use. This is where your creativity and background of rhythm playing (i.e. rhythms and techniques outlined in this book etc.) must be put to use. You should generally only attempt songs that you know well, and listen to original recordings of these songs to gain rhythm ideas.

Accessories...

The Capo

The capo is a device which is placed across the neck of the guitar (acting as a moveable nut). This enables you to change the key of a song without changing the chord shapes. It also allows you to play easier chord shapes for songs in difficult keys. To learn how to use a capo, see Complete Learn to Play Rhythm Guitar or Complete Learn to Play Fingerpicking Guitar.

Appendix Four - Transposing

The term 'Transposing' is used to describe the process whereby a progression (or song) is changed from one key to another. This is done for two main reasons:

1. Singing - to sing the whole song at a lower or higher pitch (depending on the singer's vocal range).
2. Ease of playing - because of the musical structure of the guitar, some keys are easier to play in than others. For example, beginning students may not be able to play a song in the key of E♭, but could perhaps play it in the key of C.

Consider the following turnaround in the key of C:

C   **Am**   **Dm**   **G⁷**

If you needed to transpose this progression into the key of G, the following method may be used:

1. Write out the C chromatic* scale.
2. Write out the G chromatic scale, with each note directly below its counterpart in the C chromatic scale, as such:

3. When the given progression is transposed to the key of G, the first chord, C major, will become G major. This can be seen by relating the two chromatic scales via arrow one.
4. The second chord of the progression, Am, will become Em (arrow 2). Although the name will change when transposing, its **type** (i.e. major, minor seventh etc.) will remain the same.
5. The complete transposition will be:

Key of C:

C   **Am**   **Dm**   **G⁷**

Key of G:

G   **Em**   **Am**   **D⁷**

Play both progressions and notice the similarity in sound.

* See Glossary

In the early stages you will mainly transpose for ease of playing, and thus the easiest keys for a song to be transposed into are C, G and D (for major keys) and Am, Em and Bm (for minor keys). Remember to write the second chromatic scale directly under the first, note for note, in order to transpose correctly. Try transposing the previous progression into the key of D major.

The Capo

The capo is a device which is placed across the neck of the guitar (acting as a moveable nut). It has 2 uses:

1. To enable the use of easier chord shapes, without changing the key of a song.
2. To change the key of a song into a key which is within your singing range, but involves difficult chord shapes (e.g. in the key of E♭), a capo may be used to simplify the chord shapes.

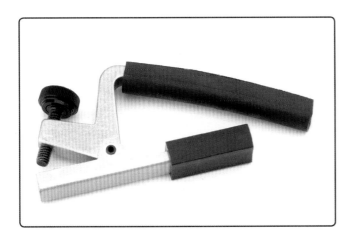

Capos come in various shapes and sizes.

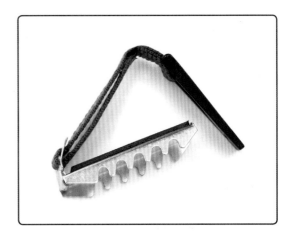

The capo allows you to play the song in the same key, yet at the same time use easier (open) chords. Consider a turnaround in E♭:

If you place the capo on the third fret, the following chords can be played without changing the song's key.

| C | Am | F | G |

If you place the capo on the third fret, the following chords can be played without changing the song's key.

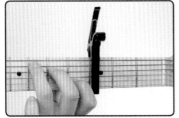

(C chord shape with capo)

(Am chord shape with capo)

(F chord shape with capo)

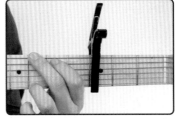

(G chord shape with capo)

If you have studied bar chords, you will notice that the capo is acting as a bar.
To work out which fret the capo must be placed on, simply count the number of semitones between the 'capo' key you have selected to change to.* For example C, as used in the above example and the original key (That is E♭ as above). Hence C to E♭ = 3 semitones, and therefore the capo must be placed on the third fret. Expanding upon point 2, consider a song in the key of C, using the turnaround progression:

A singer may decide that this key is unsuitable for his or her voice range and may wish to use the key of, say, E♭. The progression, transposed to E♭, will become:

Instead of changing to these new chord shapes (that is having to use bar chords), the guitarist may still play the C, Am, F and G chords, but must place the capo at the 3rd fret to do so.

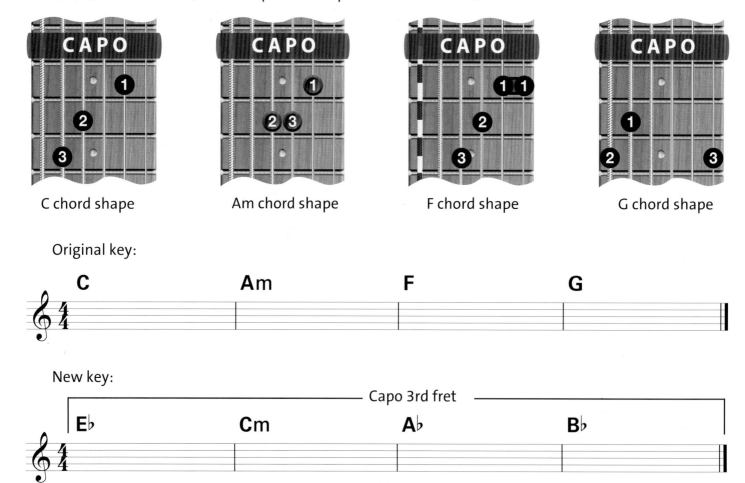

* Remember you are not actually changing key but merely the chord shapes, for ease of playing.

Appendix Five- Playing in a Band

A successful group is not just a mixture of good musicians. You will need to be aware of the many other factors involved in order to avoid the pitfalls that cause many groups to disband within a very short time. The following ideas should increase your awareness of the problems facing a group, and how to avoid them.

1. **Group Direction**

   Before forming a group, you should talk with prospective musicians about their aims for the group. You may decide to form what is called a '60/40' group; the type that plays at cabarets, dances and hotels. This type of group plays a selection of old pop standards (approximately 60%) and 'Top 40' tunes (40%). 60/40 groups can be assured of a steady income, although recognition will not go beyond the local playing scene.

   A different aim for the group may be to play mainly original material in the eventual hope of cutting a record and going on tours. Groups of this type generally do not make much money until they have become well known.

   If you are forming a new group you may find it beneficial to play a 60/40 style to gain experience and money to invest in top quality equipment.

   Decide on the number of musicians, the type of instruments and the basic style of music before forming the group.

2. **Music Choice**

   The style of music you play must be one that is enjoyed by all group members (note just a majority vote). Listen to other bands playing their various different styles and take particular note of the audience reaction in order to gauge the appeal of each style. Once you have decided on a style, aim specifically towards the section of people who enjoy that type of music. This will immediately decrease the number of possible venues for you to play at; but remember that you cannot please everyone and you should therefore aim to play to the type of people whom you will please.

3. **The Group Structure**

   A group can be divided into 2 basic sections; a 'rhythm section' and a 'lead section'. The instruments of the rhythm section include drums, bass (which lay down the basic beat), and rhythm guitar (which 'fills-out' the basic beat). These instruments must co-ordinate to provide the background rhythm; the 'tightness' of the group will depend on it.

   The lead section usually consists of lead guitar, vocals and keyboards (which may be used as either a lead or rhythm instrument). The lead instrument acts as a separate voice from the vocals and 'leads' in and out of each section or verse of a song (such as an introduction or a 'lead break').

   All instruments must work as a team, in order to provide a combined group sound.

4. **Rehearsals**

   In a serious group you will spend more time rehearsing than doing anything else, so it is important to be properly organised. As far as possible, each session should have an objective which you should strive to achieve.

   Remember that the performance of a song involves not only the music, but also sound balance and stage presentation. These facets should be practiced as part of the rehearsal.

   As well as group rehearsal, you should practice individually. Concentrate particularly on the harder sections of your songs, so that it will be easier to play them when working with the group. It is far more beneficial and time saving for each member to attend group practice with full knowledge of his part.

The underlying theme of all the above topics is one of group unity, both on and off the stage. This is essential if the group is to survive together as an effective musical unit.

Appendix Six
Chord Formula Chart

The following chart gives a comprehensive list of chord formulas, together with an example based on the **C Scale**:

CHORD NAME	CHORD FORMULA	EXAMPLE	
Major	1 3 5	C:	C E G
Suspended	1 4 5	Csus:	C F G
Major add Ninth	1 3 5 9	Cadd9:	C E G D
Minor	1 ♭3 5	Cm:	C E♭ G
Augmented	1 3 ♯5	Caug:	C E G♯
Major Sixth	1 3 5 6	C6:	C E G A
Major Sixth add Ninth	1 3 5 6 9	C6/9:	C E G A D
Minor Sixth	1 ♭3 5 6	Cm6:	C E♭ G A
Minor Sixth add Ninth	1 ♭3 5 6 9	Cm6/9:	C E♭ G A D
Seventh	1 3 5 ♭7	C7:	C E G B♭
Seventh Suspended	1 4 5 ♭7	C7sus:	C F G B♭
Minor Seventh	1 ♭3 5 ♭7	Cm7:	C E♭ G B♭
Diminished Seventh	1 ♭3 ♭5 ♭♭7	Cdim:	C E♭ G♭ B♭♭ (A)
Major Seventh	1 3 5 7	Cmaj7:	C E G B
Minor Major Seventh	1 ♭3 5 7	Cm(maj7):	C E♭ G B
Ninth	1 3 5 ♭7 9	C9:	C E G B♭ D
Minor Ninth	1 ♭3 5 ♭7 9	Cm9:	C E♭ G B♭ D
Major Ninth	1 3 5 7 9	Cmaj9:	C E G B D
Eleventh	1 3* 5 ♭7 9 11	C11:	C E* G B♭ D F
Minor Eleventh	1 ♭3 5 ♭7 9 11	Cm11:	C E♭ G B♭ D F
Thirteenth	1 3* 5 ♭7 9 11* 13	C13:	C E* G B♭ D F* A
Minor Thirteenth	1 ♭3 5 ♭7 9 11* 13	Cm13:	C E♭ G B♭ D F* A

*indicates that a note is optional.

A **double flat** ♭♭, lowers the note's pitch by **one tone**. A **double sharp** x, raises the note's pitch by **one tone**. The above chart lists chord formulas for all the different chord types learned and a few additional ones. This is how it works:

B7 is based on the dominant 7th formula ($\bar{\text{I}}$ - $\overline{\text{III}}$ - $\bar{\text{V}}$ - ♭$\overline{\text{VII}}$), and the B scale:

B   C♯   D♯   E   F♯   G♯   A♯   B

Thus: $\bar{\text{I}}$ $\overline{\text{III}}$ $\bar{\text{V}}$ ♭$\overline{\text{VII}}$

B   D♯   F♯   A

Major scales not studied in this book can be derived by following the interval sequence tone - tone - semitone - tone - tone - tone - semitone. (See Lesson 23).

Altered Chords

Other chords that you will occasionally see in sheet music involve a slight alteration to one of the given formulas. The alteration is usually indicated in the name given to the chord. Consider the following examples:

C7:	C E	G♭	B

C7♭5:	C E♭	G♭	B

The C7♭5 chord is just as the name implies; a C7 chord with the fifth note flattened.

G9:	G	B	D	F	A
G7♯9:	G	B	D	F	A♯

The G7♯9 chord involves sharpening the 9th note of the G9 chord. Another type of alteration occurs when chord symbols are written thus:

Example 1: G/F♯ bass. This indicates that a G chord is played, but using as F♯ note in the bass.
Example 2: C/G bass. This indicates a C chord with a G bass note. Sometimes the word 'bass' will not be written (i.e. the symbol will be just G/F♯), but the same meaning is implied.

Scale Tone Chords

In any given key certain chords are more common than others. For example, in the key of C the chords, C, F and G are usually present, and quite often the chords Am, Dm and Em occur. The reason for this is that each key has its own set of chords, which are constructed from notes of its own major scale. These chords are referred to as 'scale tone' chords.
Consider the C major scale:

C	D	E	F	G	A	B	C
I̲	I̲I̲	I̲I̲I̲	I̲V̲	V̲	V̲I̲	V̲I̲I̲	V̲I̲I̲I̲

Chords are constructed by combining notes which are a third apart. For example, consider the formula for a major chord:

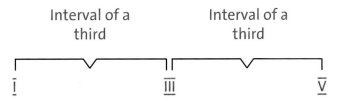

Using the C major scale written above, scale tone chords can be constructed by placing 2 third intervals above each note. This is illustrated in the following table:

V̲	G	A	B	C	D	E	F	G	} Third interval
I̲I̲I̲	E	F	G	A	B	C	D	E	} Third interval
C Scale:	C	D	E	F	G	A	B	C	
Chord constructed:	C	Dm	Em	F	G	Am	B°	C	

Notice that the chords are named according to their root note (and hence use the root note's scale). However, they are all C scale tone chords because they contain only notes of the C scale (i.e. no sharps or flats).

The method used for constructing scale tone chords in the key of C may be applied to any major scale. The result will always produce the following scale tone chords:

Scale note:	I̲	I̲I̲	III	IV	V	VI	VII	VIII
Chord constructed:	major	minor	minor	major	major	minor	diminished	major

Thus in the key of G major, the scale tone chords will be:

G	Am	Bm	C	D	Em	F♯°	G

and in the key of E♭ major, the scale tone chords will be:

E♭	Fm	Gm	A♭	B♭	Cm	D°	E♭

Scale Tone Chord Extensions

The scale tone chords studied so far involve the placement of two notes (separated by an interval of a third) above a root note. This method of building scale tone chords can be extended by adding another note, illustrated in the following table:

VII	B	C	D	E	F	G	A	B	
V̲	G	A	B	C	D	E	F	G	} Third interval
III	E	F	G	A	B	C	D	E	} Third interval
C Scale:	C	D	E	F	G	A	B	C	} Third interval
Chord constructed:	Cmaj7	Dm7	Em7	Fmaj7	G7	Am7	B∅7*	Cmaj7	

From this example, the scale tone chords for any key will be:

I̲	I̲I̲	III	IV	V	VI	VII	VIII
maj7	m7	m7	maj7	dom7	m7	∅7	maj7

*This is the symbol for a half-diminished chord (∅)

G half diminished
G∅7

(Root 6)

B half diminished
B∅7

(Root 5)

Glossary of Musical Terms

Accidental — a sign used to show a temporary change in pitch of a note (i.e. sharp♯, flat♭, double sharp ✕, double flat ♭♭, or natural ♮). The sharps or flats in a key signature are not regarded as accidentals.

Ad lib — to be played at the performer's own discretion.

Allegretto — moderately fast.

Allegro — fast and lively.

Anacrusis — a note or notes occurring before the first bar of music (also called 'lead-in' notes).

Andante — an easy walking pace.

Arpeggio — the playing of a chord in single note fashion.

Bar — a division of music occurring between two bar lines (also called a 'measure').

Bar chord — a chord played with one finger lying across all six strings.

Bar line — a vertical line drawn across the staff which divides the music into equal sections called bars.

Bass — the lower regions of pitch in general. On keyboard, the notes to the left of the keyboard.

Capo — a device placed across the neck of a guitar to allow a key change without alteration of the chord shapes.

Chord — a combination of three or more different notes played together.

Chord progression — a series of chords played as a musical unit (e.g. as in a song).

Chromatic scale — a scale ascending and descending in semitones.

e.g. **C** chromatic scale:

ascending: C   C♯   D   D♯   E   F   F♯   G   G♯   A   A♯   B   C

descending: C   B   B♭   A   A♭   G   G♭   F   E   E♭   D   D♭   C

Clef — a sign placed at the beginning of each staff of music which fixes the location of a particular note on the staff, and hence the location of all other notes, e.g.

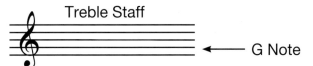

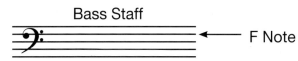

Coda — an ending section of music, signified by the sign ⊕ .

Common time — and indication of ₄₄ time — four quarter note beats per bar (also indicated by 𝄴)

D.C. al fine — a repeat from the sign (indicated thus 𝄋) to the word 'fine'.

Duration — the time value of each note.

Dynamics — the varying degrees of softness (indicated by the term 'piano') and loudness (indicated by the term 'forte') in music.

Eighth note — a note with the value of half a beat in ₄₄ time, indicated thus ♪ (also called a quaver).

The eighth note rest — indicating half a beat of silence is written: 𝄾

Glossary of Musical Terms - Continued (1)

Enharmonic — describes the difference in notation, but not in pitch, of two notes: e.g.

F♯ or G♭

Fermata — a sign, ⌢ , used to indicate that a note or chord is held to the player's own discretion (also called a 'pause sign').

First and second endings — signs used where two different endings occur. On the first time through ending one is played (indicated by the bracket ⌐1. ⌐); then the progression is repeated and ending two is played (indicated ⌐2. ⌐).

Flat — a sign, (♭)used to lower the pitch of a note by one semitone.

Forte — loud. Indicated by the sign *f* .

Half note — a note with the value of two beats in 𝄴 time, indicated thus: ♩ (also called a minim). The half note rest, indicating two beats of silence, is written: ▬ on the third staff line.

Harmonics — a chime like sound created by lightly touching a vibrating string at certain points along the fret board.

Harmony — the simultaneous sounding of two or more different notes.

Improvise — to perform spontaneously; i.e. not from memory or from a written copy.

Interval — the distance between any two notes of different pitches.

Key — describes the notes used in a composition in regards to the major or minor scale from which they are taken; e.g. a piece 'in the key of C major' describes the melody, chords, etc., as predominantly consisting of the notes, **C, D, E, F, G, A,** and **B** — i.e. from the **C** scale.

Key signature — a sign, placed at the beginning of each stave of music, directly after the clef, to indicate the key of a piece. The sign consists of a certain number of sharps or flats, which represent the sharps or flats found in the scale of the piece's key. e.g.

 indicates a scale with **F♯** and **C♯**, which is **D** major; **D E F♯ G A B C♯ D**. Therefore the key is **D** major (or its relative minor, B).

Lead-In — same as anacrusis (also called a pick-up).

Leger lines — small horizontal lines upon which notes are written when their pitch is either above or below the range of the staff, e.g.

Legato — smoothly, well connected.

Lyric — words that accompany a melody.

Major scale — a series of eight notes in alphabetical order based on the interval sequence tone - tone - semitone - tone - tone - tone - semitone, giving the familiar sound **do re mi fa so la ti do**.

Melody — a succession of notes of varying pitch and duration, and having a recognizable musical shape.

Metronome — a device which indicates the number of beats per minute, and which can be adjusted in accordance to the desired tempo.

e.g. **MM** (Maelzel Metronome) ♩= 60 — indicates 60 quarter note beats per minute.

Moderato — at a moderate pace.

Glossary of Musical Terms - Continued (2)

Natural — a sign (♮)used to cancel out the effect of a sharp or flat. The word is also used to describe the notes **A, B, C, D, E, F** and **G**; e.g. 'the natural notes'.

Notation — the written representation of music, by means of symbols (music on a staff), letters (as in chord and note names) and diagrams (as in chord illustrations.)

Note — a single sound with a given pitch and duration.

Octave — the distance between any given note with a set frequency, and another note with exactly double that frequency. Both notes will have the same letter name;

Open chord — a chord that contains at least one open string.

Pitch — the sound produced by a note, determined by the frequency of the string vibrations. The pitch relates to a note being referred to as 'high' or 'low'.

Plectrum — a small object (often of a triangular shape)made of plastic which is used to pick or strum the strings of a guitar.

Position — a term used to describe the location of the left hand on the fret board. The left hand position is determined by the fret location of the first finger, e.g. The 1st position refers to the 1st to 4th frets. The 3rd position refers to the 3rd to 6th frets and so on.

Quarter note — a note with the value of one beat in $\frac{4}{4}$ time, indicated thus ♩ (also called a crotchet). The quarter note rest, indicating one beat of silence, is written: 𝄽.

Repeat signs — in music, used to indicate a repeat of a section of music, by means of two dots placed before a double bar line:

In chord progressions, a repeat sign ✗, indicates an exact repeat of the previous bar.

Rhythm — the natural pattern of strong and weak pulses in a piece of music.

Riff — a pattern of notes that is repeated throughout a progression (song).

Root note — the note after which a chord or scale is named.

Scale Tone Chords — chords which are constructed from notes within a given scale.

Semitone — the smallest interval used in conventional music. On guitar, it is a distance of one fret.

Sharp — a sign (♯) used to raise the pitch of a note by one semitone.

Simple time — occurs when the beat falls on an undotted note, which is thus divisible by two.

Sixteenth note — a note with the value of a quarter of a beat in $\frac{4}{4}$ time, indicated as such ♬ (also called a semiquaver).
The sixteenth note rest, indicating a quarter of a beat of silence, is written: 𝄾

Slide — a technique which involves a finger moving along the string to its new note. The finger maintains pressure on the string, so that a continuous sound is produced.

Slur — sounding a note by using only the left hand fingers. (An ascending slur is also called a 'hammer on'; a descending slur is also called a 'pull off.')

Staccato — to play short and detached. Indicated by a dot placed above the note:

Glossary of Musical Terms - Continued (3)

Staff — five parallel lines together with four spaces, upon which music is written.

Syncopation — the placing of an accent on a normally unaccented beat. e.g.:

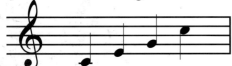 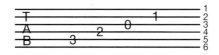

Tablature — a system of writing music which represents the position of the player's fingers (not the pitch of the notes, but their position on the guitar). A chord diagram is a type of tablature. Notes can also be written using tablature thus:

 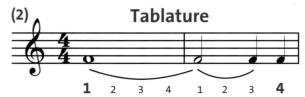

Tempo — the speed of a piece.

Tie — a curved line joining two or more notes of the same pitch, where the second note(s) is not played, but its time value is added to that of the first note.

(1) Music Notation	(2) Tablature

Timbre — a quality which distinguishes a note produced on one instrument from the same note produced on any other instrument (also called 'tone colour'). A given note on the guitar will sound different (and therefore distinguishable) from the same pitched note on piano, violin, flute etc. There is usually also a difference in timbre from one guitar to another.

Time signature — a sign at the beginning of a piece which indicates, by means of figures, the number of beats per bar (top figure), and the type of note receiving one beat (bottom figure).

Tone — a distance of two frets; i.e. the equivalent of two semitones.

Transposition — the process of changing music from one key to another.

Treble — the upper regions of pitch in general.

Treble clef — a sign placed at the beginning of the staff to fix the pitch of the notes placed on it. The treble clef (also called 'G clef') is placed so that the second line indicates as G note:

 ← G line

Tremolo (pick motion) — a technique involving rapid pick movement on a given note.

Triplet — a group of three notes played in the same time as two notes of the same kind.

Vibrato — a technique which involves pushing a string up and down, like a rapid series of short bends.

Wedge mark — indicates pick direction;

> e.g: V = down pick,   Λ = up pick

Whole note — a note with the value of four beats in 4/4 time, indicated thus O (also called a semibreve).